Myth: A Very Short Introduction

'This crisp little volume packs an awful lot into a small package. Its extensive list of short surveys of primary approaches to myth will be useful to the beginning student.'

Ivan Strenski, Professor of Religious Studies, University of California Riverside

'A concise, precise, erudite and insightful analysis of myth, a central concept that has haunted human thought and belief—and theories about them—from classical philosophy to modern social and cultural theories.'

Dan Ben-Amos, Department of Near Eastern Languages and Civilizations, University of Pennsylvania

VERY SHORT INTRODUCTIONS are for anyone wanting a stimulating and accessible way into a new subject. They are written by experts, and have been translated into more than 40 different languages.

The series began in 1995, and now covers a wide variety of topics in every discipline. The VSI library now contains over 400 volumes—a Very Short Introduction to everything from Psychology and Philosophy of Science to American History and Relativity—and continues to grow in every subject area.

Very Short Introductions available now:

Available soon:

For more information visit our website

www.oup.com/vsi/

Robert A. Segal

MYTH

A Very Short Introduction

SECOND EDITION

OXFORD
UNIVERSITY PRESS

OXFORD

UNIVERSITY PRESS

Great Clarendon Street, Oxford, OX2 6DP,
United Kingdom

Oxford University Press is a department of the University of Oxford.
It furthers the University's objective of excellence in research, scholarship,
and education by publishing worldwide. Oxford is a registered trade mark of
Oxford University Press in the UK and in certain other countries

First edition published 2004
Second edition published 2015

Impression: 10

Published in the United States of America by Oxford University Press
198 Madison Avenue, New York, NY 10016, United States of America

British Library Cataloguing in Publication Data

Data available

Library of Congress Control Number: 2015931933

ISBN 978-0-19-872470-4

Printed in Great Britain by
Ashford Colour Press Ltd, Gosport, Hampshire

In memory of Skip, Misty, and Spud,
three beloved cats

Contents

List of illustrations

Introduction: theories of myth

This book is an introduction to approaches to myth, or theories of myth, and it is limited to modern theories. Theories of myth may be as old as myths themselves. Certainly they go back to the Presocratics. But only modern theories—theories from the 19th century on—have purported to be scientific. For only since then have there existed the social sciences, of which anthropology, psychology, and sociology have contributed the most to the study of myth. Where earlier theorizing was largely speculative and abstract, scientific theorizing is based far more on accumulated information. Undeniably, some important modern theories of myth hail from the hoary disciplines of philosophy and literature, but they, too, reflect the influence of the social sciences.

Strictly, theories of myth are theories of some much larger domain. Anthropological theories of myth are theories of culture *applied* to the case of myth. Psychological theories of myth are theories of the mind. Sociological theories of myth are theories of society. There are no theories of myth alone, however broadly the term myth is sometimes used. Myth is not like literature, which, so it has or had traditionally been claimed, must be studied as *literature* rather than as history, sociology, or something else non-literary.

What unites the study of myth across the disciplines are the questions asked. The three main questions are those of origin, function, and subject matter. By 'origin' is meant both why and how myth arises. By 'function' is meant both why and how myth persists. The answer to the why of origin and function is usually a need, which myth arises to fulfil and lasts by continuing to fulfil. What the need is, varies from theory to theory. By 'subject matter' is meant the referent of myth. Some theories read myth literally, so that the referent is the straightforward, apparent one, such as gods. Other theories read myth symbolically, and what is symbolized are most often natural phenomena or human attributes.

Theories differ not only in their answers to these questions but also in the questions they ask. Some theories and some disciplines concentrate on the origin of myth; others, on the function; still others, on the subject matter. Only a few theories address all three questions, and some of the theories that address origin or function deal with either 'why' or 'how' but not both.

The conventional view is that theories of the 19th century focused on the origin of myth and that theories since then have focused on the function and subject matter. But this characterization confuses historical origin with recurrent origin. Theories that profess to provide the origin of myth claim to know not where and when myth first arose but why and how myth arises wherever and whenever it does. The issue of recurrent origin has been as popular with contemporary theories as with 19th-century ones, and interest in function and subject matter was as common to 19th-century theories as to subsequent ones. Furthermore, the why of origin and function is the same.

There is one genuine difference between 19th-century theories and subsequent ones. Nineteenth-century theories tended to see the subject matter of myth as the physical world and to see the function of myth as a literal explanation of that world. Myth was typically taken to be the primitive counterpart to science, which was assumed to be largely or even wholly modern. Science rendered myth not merely redundant but outright incompatible, so that moderns, who by definition are scientific, had to reject myth. By contrast, subsequent theories have tended to see myth as almost anything but an outdated counterpart to science, either in subject matter or in function. Consequently, moderns are not obliged to abandon myth for science. (Friedrich Nietzsche, who died in 1900, was in effect a subsequent theorist ahead of his time.)

Besides the questions of origin, function, and subject matter, questions often asked about myth include: Is myth universal? Is myth true? The answers to these questions stem from the answers to the first three questions. A theory which maintains that myth functions to explain physical processes is committed to the falsity of myth if the explanation given proves incompatible with a scientific one. A theory which maintains that myth functions to unify society may circumvent the issue of truth by asserting that society is unified when its members simply *believe* that the laws they are expected to obey were established long ago by revered ancestors.

Definition of myth

I propose defining myth as a story—a term that I will later distinguish from text and narrative but that for now I will use in its everyday sense. That myth, whatever else it is, is a story may seem self-evident. Yet myth can also be taken more broadly as a conviction or credo—for example, the American 'rags to riches myth' and the American 'myth of the frontier'. In the 19th century Horatio Alger wrote scores of popular novels illustrating the rags to riches myth, but the myth already existed and continues even after the fading of Alger's popularity. (For the record, riches come to his subjects not from working hard but from doing something courageous or honest for a wealthy man, who then adopts the boy.) Likewise the myth of the frontier stands independent of any stories that exemplify it.

3

Still, I propose requiring that myth be a story, and all of the theories considered in this book deem it so. True, Claude Lévi-Strauss ventures beyond the story to the 'structure' of myth, but the structure is conveyed by the story. Theories that read myth symbolically rather than literally still take the subject matter, or the meaning, to be the unfolding of a story.

If, then, myth is to be taken here as a story, what is the story about? For folklorists, whose position is the narrowest, myth is about the creation of the world. In the Bible only the two creation stories (Genesis 1 and 2), the Garden of Eden story (Genesis 3), and the Noah story (Genesis 6–9) would thereby qualify as myths. All the other stories would instead constitute either legends or folk tales. Outside the Bible the Oedipus 'myth', for example, would actually be a legend. I do not propose being so rigid and will instead define myth as simply a story about something significant. The story can take place in the past, as Mircea Eliade and Bronislaw Malinowski insist, or in the present or the future.

For theories from, above all, religious studies, the main characters in myth must be gods or near-gods. Here, too, I do not propose being so rigid. If I were, I would have to exclude most of the Hebrew Bible, in which all the stories may *involve* God but, apart from only the first two chapters of Genesis, are at least as much about human beings as about God. I will insist only that the main figures be personalities—divine, human, or even animal. Excluded would be impersonal forces such as Plato's Good. Among theorists, E. B. Tylor is the most preoccupied with the personalistic nature of myth, but all the other theorists to be discussed assume it—with the exception of Lévi-Strauss. At the same time the personalities can be either the agents or the objects of actions.

Save for Rudolf Bultmann and Hans Jonas, all of the theorists considered address the function of myth, and Malinowski focuses on it. Theorists differ over what the function of myth is. I do not propose dictating what the function must be. I note only that for all the theorists the function is weighty—in contrast to the lighter functions of legend and folk tale. I thereby propose that myth accomplishes something significant for adherents, but I leave open what that accomplishment might be. And again, the need that myth functions to fulfil is the same as the need that myth originates to fulfil.

In today's parlance, myth is false. Myth is 'mere' myth. There abound books entitled Celebrity X: The Myth and the Reality. In 1997 historian William Rubinstein published *The Myth of Rescue: Why the Democracies Could Not Have Saved More Jews from the Nazis*. The title is self-evident. The book challenges the common conviction that many Jewish victims of the Nazis could have been saved if only the Allies had cared. Rubinstein is challenging the assumption that the Allies were indifferent to the fate of European Jews and were indifferent because they were anti-Semitic. For him, the term 'myth' captures the sway of the conviction about the failure to rescue more fully than would tamer phrases like 'erroneous belief' and 'popular misconception'. For him, a 'myth' is a conviction false yet tenacious.

By contrast, the phrase 'rags to riches myth' uses the term myth positively yet still conveys the grip of the conviction. A blatantly false conviction might seem to have a stronger hold than a true one, for the conviction remains firm even in the face of its transparent falsity. But a cherished conviction that is true can be clutched as tightly as a false one. Ironically, some Americans who continue to espouse the rags to riches credo may no longer call it a 'myth' *because* the term has come to connote falsity. I propose that, to qualify as a myth, a story, which can of course express a conviction, must have a powerful hold on its adherents. But the story can be either true or false.

The myth of Adonis

In order to compare theories, I propose taking a familiar myth—that of Adonis—and applying theories to it. The main sources of the myth are the Greek Apollodorus' *Library* (Book III, chapter 14, paragraphs 3–4) and the Roman Ovid's *Metamorphoses* (Book X, lines 298–739).

According to Apollodorus, who himself cites a version of the story from the epic poet Panyasis, Adonis' mother, Smyrna, was irresistibly attracted to her father and became pregnant with his child. When her father discovered that it was Smyrna with whom he had nightly been having sex, he immediately drew his sword. She fled, and he pursued her. On the verge of being overtaken, she prayed to the gods to become invisible, and they, taking pity, turned her into a myrrh (smyrna) tree. Ten months later the tree burst open, and Adonis was born.

Even as an infant, Adonis was preternaturally beautiful, and Aphrodite, who apparently had kept watch over him, was irresistibly smitten with him, just as Smyrna had been with her father. To have him all to herself, Aphrodite hid Adonis in a chest. When Persephone, queen of the Underworld (Hades), opened the chest, which Aphrodite had entrusted to her without revealing its contents, she too fell in love with Adonis and refused to return him to Aphrodite. Each goddess wanted Adonis exclusively for herself. The king of the gods, Zeus, was appealed to by both sides in Solomonic fashion, and he ruled that Adonis should spend a third of the year with Persephone, a third with Aphrodite, and a third alone. Adonis readily ceded his third to Aphrodite and was thereby never outside the custody of a goddess. One day, while hunting, he was gored to death by a boar. According to another, unnamed version of the story recounted by Apollodorus, the goring was the work of Ares, god of war, who was angry at having been bested by Adonis as the lover of Aphrodite.

Ovid similarly takes the story of Adonis back to incest between his mother, Myrrha, and her father, here Cinyras. Myrrha was on the point of hanging herself to be free from her distress when she was saved by her old nurse, who pried loose the source of Myrrha's despair and, as in Apollodorus, arranged for Myrrha to bed her father without discovery. But when, on the third night, he called for light to discover who it was who loved him so, he, as in Apollodorus, drew his sword, and she fled. For nine months the pregnant Myrrha wandered. Also as in Apollodorus, the worn-out Myrrha prayed and was turned by the pitying gods into a tree—though here at the end, not the beginning, of her pregnancy. Yet Myrrha remained human enough to weep, and from her tears came the perfume myrrh. The baby, still alive in her, had to fight its way out of the tree to be born.

In Ovid, in contrast to Apollodorus, Venus (the Roman name for Aphrodite) encountered Adonis only as a young man but was likewise immediately smitten. There was no rivalry with other goddesses, so that Venus had him all to herself. They went hunting together (see Figure 1). While Venus continually warned him to stick to small game, he heedlessly took on big game and, as in Apollodorus' version, was gored to death by a boar, though not one sent by any rival for Venus' love.

Where Apollodorus' story ends with Adonis' death, Ovid's continues with Venus' mourning for him. As a memorial, she sprinkled nectar over his blood, from which sprouted the flower anemone. Like Adonis, it is short-lived.

Where for Apollodorus the annual cycle of death and rebirth *antedates* Adonis' 'final' death, for Ovid the annual cycle, in the form of the flower, *follows* Adonis' death. The planting of the flower anticipates the ritual associated with the myth of Adonis—a connection absent from Apollodorus.

Where for Apollodorus the main spur to events is anger, for Ovid it is love. Where for Apollodorus Adonis is the innocent victim

1. Venus and Adonis by Rubens.

of warring parents and of rival deities, for Ovid the inconsolable Aphrodite is as much the victim as Adonis.

Where Apollodorus presents the story as true, Ovid presents it as fictional. Where Apollodorus tells it straight, Ovid twists it to fit larger themes—notably, that of transformation, as in Myrrha's becoming a tree and Adonis' becoming a flower. Where Apollodorus intends his story to be taken literally, Ovid intends his to be read metaphorically.

Applying theories to myths

Theorizing about myth is not optional. It is inescapable. For example, handbooks of classical mythology that matter-of-factly connect Adonis' annual trek to Persephone and return to Aphrodite with the course of vegetation presuppose a view of myth as the primitive counterpart to science.

Theories need myths as much as myths need theories. If theories illuminate myths, myths confirm theories. True, the sheer applicability of a myth does not itself confirm the theory, the tenets of which must be established in their own right. For example, to show that Jung's theory, when applied, elucidates the myth of Adonis would not itself establish the existence of a collective unconscious, which, on the contrary, would be presupposed. But one, albeit indirect, way of confirming a theory is to show how well it works *when* its tenets are assumed—this on the grounds that the theory must be either false or limited if it turns out not to work.

For the revised edition of this book I have made many changes, above all the addition of the myth of Gaia as a possible way of reconciling myth with science. The chapter 'myth and society' is now the chapter 'myth and politics'. I have also dropped the placing of quotation marks around 'primitive' to acknowledge, which instead I do here, the inappropriateness today of a term used by theorists in the past.

Chapter 1
Myth and science

In the West the challenge to myth goes back at least to Plato, who rejected Homeric myth on, especially, ethical grounds. It was above all the Stoics who defended myth against this charge by reinterpreting it allegorically. The chief modern challenge to myth has come not from ethics but from science. Here myth is assumed to explain how gods control the physical world rather than, as for Plato, to describe how they behave among themselves. Where Plato bemoans myths for presenting the gods as practitioners of immoral behaviour, modern critics dismiss myth for explaining the world unscientifically.

Myth as true science

One form of the modern challenge to myth has been to the scientific credibility of myth. Did creation really occur in a mere six days, as the first of two creation stories in Genesis (1:1–2:4a) claims? Was there really a worldwide flood? Is the earth truly but six or seven thousand years old? Could the ten plagues on the Egyptians actually have happened? The most unrepentant defence against this challenge has been to claim that the biblical account of these events is correct, for, after all, the Pentateuch was revealed to Moses by God. Taking the Bible as the inerrant, literal word of God is the position known as fundamentalism. Close to it is the more flexible position known as 'creationism', which ranges, for example, from taking the days of creation to mean literally six days to taking them symbolically to mean 'ages'. Fundamentalism and creationism arose in reaction to Darwin's *Origin of Species* (1859), which contends that species gradually emerged out of one another rather than being created separately and virtually simultaneously. Surprisingly, creationism has become ever more, not ever less, uncompromisingly literalist in its rendition of the biblical account of creation.

At the same time creationists of all stripes vaunt their views as scientific *as well as* religious and not, as with fundamentalism, as religious *rather than* scientific. 'Creationism' is shorthand for 'creation science', which appropriates scientific evidence of any kind both to bolster its own claims and to refute those of secular rivals like evolution. Doubtless 'creation scientists' would object to the term 'myth' to characterize the view they defend, but only because the term has come to connote false belief. If the term is used neutrally for a staunchly held conviction, true or false, creationism is a myth that claims to be scientific. For creation scientists, it is evolution that is untenable scientifically. In any clash between the Bible and modern science, modern science must give way to biblical science, not vice versa.

Myth as modern science

A much tamer defence against the challenge of modern science has been to reconcile myth with that science. Here science means modern science. There is no mythic or religious science. Elements at odds with modern science are either removed or, more cleverly, reinterpreted as in fact modern and scientific. Myth is credible scientifically because it *is* science, of which there is only one kind. There might not have been a Noah able singlehandedly to gather up all living species and to keep them alive in a wooden boat sturdy enough to withstand the strongest seas that ever arose, but a worldwide flood did occur. What thus remains in myth is true because it is scientific. This approach is the opposite of that called 'demythologizing', which *separates* myth from science. Demythologizing will be considered in Chapter 2.

Myths about not only floods but also volcanoes and earthquakes have been interpreted as records of actual events. In *Natural Knowledge in Preclassical Antiquity* Mott Greene correlates the divine war in Hesiod's *Theogony* with a volcanic eruption. In *When They Severed Earth from Sky* Elizabeth Barber and Paul Barber match a Native American myth of a cosmic battle between gods with, again, a volcanic eruption. Myths about stars and planets have been taken as records of astronomical observations. In *Hamlet's Mill* Giorgio de Santillana and Hertha von Dechend demonstrate that detailed astronomical calculations underlie various myths. In *The Myth of Replacement* Thomas Worthen attributes many Indo-European myths to reactions to the unsettling observations of the precession of the equinoxes.

These contemporary works may seem like an unabashed throwback to a 19th-century approach to myth, for the subject of myth is again the physical world, and the function of myth is the relaying of indispensable information about it. But where these works aim to show that the information conveyed by myth is accurate scientifically, 19th-century works aimed to show that myth was unscientific. Still, the 'scientizing' of myth by these authors does constitute the continuation into the present of a 19th-century concern.

In their comment on the first plague, the turning of the waters of the Nile into blood (Exodus 7:14–24), the editors of the *New Oxford Annotated Bible* epitomize this scientizing approach: 'The plague of blood apparently reflects a natural phenomenon of Egypt: namely, the reddish color of the Nile at its height in the summer owing to red particles of earth or perhaps minute organisms.' Of the second plague, that of frogs (Exodus 8:1–15), the editors declare similarly: 'The mud of the Nile, after the

12

seasonal overflowing, was a natural place for frogs to generate. Egypt has been spared more frequent occurrence of this pestilence by the frog-eating bird, the ibis.' How fortuitous that the ibis must have been on holiday when Aaron stretched out his hand to produce the plague and must have just returned when Moses wanted the plague to cease! Instead of setting myth *against* science, this tactic turns myth *into* science—and not, as is fashionable today, science into myth.

Myth as primitive science

By far the most common response to the challenge of science has been to abandon myth for science. Here myth, while still an explanation of the world, is now taken as an explanation of its own kind and not as a scientific explanation in mythic guise. The issue is therefore not the scientific credibility of myth but the compatibility of myth with science. Myth is considered to be 'primitive' science—or, more precisely, the pre-scientific counterpart to science, which, as the popular explanation of the world, is assumed to be exclusively modern. Myth is here part of religion. Where religion apart from myth provides the sheer belief in gods, myth fills in the details of how gods cause events. Because myth is part of religion, the rise of science as the reigning modern explanation of physical events has consequently spelled the fall of not only religion but also myth. Because moderns by definition accept science, they cannot also have myth, and the phrase 'modern myth' is self-contradictory. Myth is a victim of the process of secularization that constitutes modernity.

The relationship between religion and science has actually been anything but uniform, and works with tendentious titles like *A History of the Warfare of Science with Theology in Christendom* express a one-sided viewpoint. Still, religion and science, and so myth and science, were more regularly opposed in the 19th century than ever since, when they have more often been reconciled.

E. B. Tylor

The pioneering English anthropologist E. B. Tylor (1832–1917) remains the classic exponent of the view that myth and science are at odds. Tylor subsumes myth under religion and in turn subsumes both religion and science under philosophy. He divides philosophy into 'primitive' and 'modern'. Primitive philosophy is identical with primitive religion. There is no primitive science. Modern philosophy, by contrast, has two divisions: religion and science. Of the two, science is by far the more important and is the modern counterpart to primitive religion. Modern religion is composed of two elements—metaphysics and ethics—neither of which is present in primitive religion. Tylor uses the term 'animism' for religion per se, modern and primitive alike, because he derives the belief in gods from the belief in souls (*anima* in Latin means soul). Gods are the souls in all physical entities *except* humans, who themselves are not gods.

Primitive religion is the primitive counterpart to science because both are explanations of the physical world. Tylor thus characterizes primitive religion as 'savage biology' and maintains that 'mechanical astronomy gradually superseded the animistic astronomy of the lower races' and that today 'biological pathology gradually supersedes animistic pathology'. The religious explanation is personalistic: the decisions of gods explain events. The scientific explanation is impersonal: mechanical laws explain events. The sciences as a whole have replaced religion as the explanation of the physical world, so that 'animistic astronomy' and 'animistic pathology' refer only to primitive, not modern, animism. Modern religion has surrendered the physical world to science and has retreated to the immaterial world, especially to the realm of life after death—that is, of the life of the soul after the death of the body. Where in primitive religion souls are deemed material, in modern religion they are deemed immaterial and are limited to human beings:

The soul has given up its ethereal substance, and become an immaterial entity, 'the shadow of a shade'. There has arisen an intellectual product whose very existence is of the deepest significance, a 'psychology' which has no longer anything to do with 'soul'. The soul's place in modern thought is in the metaphysics of religion, and its especial office there is that of furnishing an intellectual side to the religious doctrine of the future.

Similarly, where in primitive religion gods are deemed material, in modern religion they are deemed immaterial. Gods thereby cease to be agents in the physical world—Tylor assumes that physical effects must have physical causes—and religion ceases to be an explanation of the physical world. Gods are relocated from the physical world to the social world. They become models for humans, just as they should be for Plato. One now turns to the Bible to learn ethics, not physics. One reads the Bible not for the story of creation but for the Ten Commandments, just as for Plato a bowdlerized Homer would enable one to do. Jesus is to be emulated as the ideal human, not as a miracle worker. The epitome of this view was expressed by the Victorian cultural critic Matthew Arnold.

This irenic position is also like that of the late evolutionary biologist Stephen Jay Gould, for whom science, above all evolution, is compatible with religion because the two never intersect. Science explains the physical world; religion prescribes ethics and gives meaning to life:

> Science tries to document the factual character of the natural world, and to develop theories that coordinate and explain these facts. Religion, on the other hand, operates in the equally important, but utterly different, realm of human purposes, meanings, and values.

But where for Gould religion has *always* served a function different from that of science, for Tylor religion has been forced to retrain, having been made compulsorily redundant by science. And its present function is a demotion. Tylor is closer to biologist

Richard Dawkins, though Dawkins, unlike Tylor, is not prepared to grant religion even a lesser function in the wake of science.

For Tylor, the demise of religion as an explanation of the physical world has meant the demise of myth altogether, which for Tylor is thus confined to primitive religion. Even though myth is an elaboration on the belief in gods, the belief itself can survive the rise of science where somehow myth cannot. Where, then, there is 'modern religion', albeit religion shorn of its key role as explanation, there are no modern myths.

In pitting myth against science, as in pitting religion *qua* explanation against science, Tylor epitomizes the 19th-century view of myth. Ever since, the trend has been to reconcile myth as well as religion with science, so that moderns can retain myth as well as religion. Yet Tylor's view surely remains popular among lay persons and is assumed, for example, by those for whom the term 'myth' evokes stories about Greek and Roman gods.

For Tylor, science renders myth not merely superfluous but unacceptable. Why? Because the explanations that myth and science give are incompatible. It is not simply that the mythic explanation is personalistic and the scientific one impersonal. It is that both offer *direct* explanations of the *same* events. Gods operate not behind or through impersonal forces but in place of them. According to myth, the rain god, let us say, collects rain in buckets and then chooses to empty the buckets on some spot below. According to science, meteorological processes cause rain. One cannot stack the mythic account atop the scientific one because the rain god, rather than utilizing meteorological processes, acts in place of them.

Strictly, causation in myth is never entirely personalistic. The decision of the rain god to dump rain on a chosen spot below presupposes physical laws that account for the accumulation of rain in heaven, the capacity of the buckets to retain the rain, and the direction of the dumped rain. But to maintain his rigid hiatus between myth and science, Tylor would doubtless reply that myths themselves ignore physical processes and focus instead on divine decisions.

Tylor takes for granted not merely that primitives have only myth but, even more, that moderns have only science. Not coincidentally, he refers to the 'myth-making stage' of culture. Rather than an eternal phenomenon, as Mircea Eliade, C. G. Jung, and Joseph Campbell grandly proclaim, myth for Tylor is merely a passing, if slowly passing, one. Myth has admirably served its function, but its time is over. Moderns who still cling to myth have simply failed either to recognize or to concede the incompatibility of it with science. While Tylor does not date the beginning of the scientific stage, it is identical with the beginning of modernity and is therefore only a few centuries old. Dying in 1917, Tylor never quite envisioned a stage post the modern one. While Tylor's view is no longer common among theorists, there do remain 'Tylorians', of whom a recent exemplar is the American anthropologist David Bidney.

One reason Tylor pits myth against science is that he subsumes myth under religion. For him, there is no myth outside religion, even though modern religion is without myth. Because primitive religion is the counterpart to science, myth must be as well. Another reason Tylor pits myth against science is that he reads myth literally. He opposes those who read myth symbolically, poetically, or metaphorically—for him, interchangeable terms.

Opposite to Tylor stands his fellow Victorian, the German-born Sanskritist Friedrich Max Müller (1823–1900), who spent his career at Oxford. Where for Tylor moderns misread myth by taking it symbolically, for Müller ancients themselves eventually came to misread their own myths, or mythical data, by gradually taking them literally. Originally symbolic descriptions of natural phenomena came to be read as literal descriptions of the attributes of gods. For example, the sea described poetically as 'raging' was eventually taken as the characteristic of the personality responsible for the sea, and a myth was then invented to account for this characteristic. Mythology for Müller stems from the absence or near-absence in at least some Semitic languages of abstract nouns and of a neuter gender. Thus any name given the sun—say, 'the giver of warmth'—invariably turned an abstract, impersonal entity into an actual personality, and later generations invented myths to fill in the life of this male or female god.

A Tylorian approach to Adonis would see the myth as an explanation—for its own sake—of something striking that has been observed. For Tylor, Apollodorus' and Ovid's versions would offer an account of the origin of myrrh. Ovid's would, in addition, offer an account of the origin of the flower anemone. Further, Ovid's would account for the notable brevity of the lifespan of the flower, which would be symbolic of Adonis'. If one could generalize from the anemone to flowers and other vegetation, the myth could be explaining why these entities do not just die but also get reborn. For Tylor, Adonis would have to be a god, not a human being, and the myth would have to be attributing the annual course of flowers and of vegetation as a whole to his annual trip to Hades and back. Adonis' final death would be ignored. The stress would be on Adonis' power to control the natural entities for which he was responsible. The payoff of the myth would be wholly intellectual: one would know why crops behave so quirkily—dying and then coming back to life, and not once but forever.

Yet the myth itself does not connect Adonis' annual trip to the course of vegetation, though the ritual of planting seeds in the quick-growing and quick-dying 'gardens of Adonis' does. And even if the myth did link the trip to the course of vegetation, the effect on vegetation would come not from any decision on Adonis' part, as Tylor would require, but as the automatic consequence of his actions.

Moreover, much in the myth would still be left out. Tylor's theory simply cannot cover the issues of incest, love, jealousy, and sexuality. More precisely, it can do so only as motives on the part of Adonis. But in the myth they are the motives instead of the figures around him. He himself is more passive object than agent. And however miraculous the events in Adonis' life, he is still just a human being, not a god. Overall, the myth seems interested more in his relations with others than in either his or their impact on the physical world.

Tylor's theory seems geared more to a myth that is explicitly an account of the creation and, even better, the ongoing operation of physical phenomena. Take Genesis 1, which for Tylor would easily qualify as a myth by this criterion. To cite a few passages:

> And God said, 'Let the waters under the heavens be gathered together into one place, and let the dry land appear.' And it was so. God called the dry land Earth, and the waters that were gathered together he called Seas. And God saw that it was good.

> (Genesis 1:9–10)

> Then God said, 'Let us make man in our image, after our likeness; and let them have dominion over the fish of the sea, and over the birds of the air, and over the cattle, and over all the earth, and over every creeping thing that creeps upon the earth.' So God created man in his own image, in the image of God he created him; male and female he created them. And God blessed them, and God said to them, 'Be fruitful and multiply, and fill the earth and subdue it'…And God saw everything that he had made, and behold, it was very good.

> (Genesis 1:26–31)

Tylor's theory would better fit those elements of the world that not merely are set in order once and for all, such as dry land and seas, but also recur, such as rainfall, the change of seasons, and (in the story of Noah) the rainbow. Genesis 1 covers many recurrent phenomena: day and night, sun and moon, and all living things. Still, Tylor's theory would require that recurring phenomena come from the recurring decisions of gods. For Tylor, gods are to the physical world as humans are to the social world: each time they decide anew to do the same thing. They do not set up things that simply carry on, the way gods do for Bronislaw Malinowski and Eliade.

Even if Tylor's theory fitted snugly the process of creation in Genesis 1, much of the myth would remain beyond the ken of the theory. The myth does not just explain creation but also evaluates it, continually pronouncing it good. Because Tylor so insistently parallels myth to science, he allows no room in myth for morality. For him, Genesis 1 should merely explain, not assess, creation. Similarly, the story does not just explain the creation of human beings but also elevates them above the rest of creation, according them at once the right and the duty to oversee the physical world. If, further, the 'image' of God in which humans are created is more than anatomical, then here, too, Tylor's theory falls short.

Finally, even if Tylor's theory worked, what would it illuminate? What would Tylor's theory tell us that we would not know without it? One could not, in fairness, ask of Tylor what a myth *means*, for Tylor stands committed to a literal rendition of myth: a myth means what it says. Tylor's contribution would be to the origin and the function of myth. Genesis 1, he would contend, arose not from wild speculations about the world but from steady observations about recurrent, if still striking, natural processes that call for an explanation.

Tylor would find an appreciative audience among creationists—not because he would consider Genesis 1 the correct account of the origin of the world but because he would consider it *an* account, and a distinctively religious one. Tylor would offer a corrective to those 20th-century theologians who, intent on making the Bible palatable to moderns, maintain that Genesis 1 is anything but an account of creation—a view like that of Rudolf Bultmann on the New Testament, as we shall see in Chapter 2.

J. G. Frazer

Tylor's is but one view of the relationship between myth and science, or between religion and science. Closest to Tylor stands J. G. Frazer (1854–1941), the Scottish-born Cambridge classicist and fellow pioneering anthropologist. For Frazer, as for Tylor, myth is part of primitive religion; primitive religion is part of philosophy, itself universal; and primitive religion is the counterpart to natural science, itself entirely modern. Primitive religion and science are, as for Tylor, mutually exclusive. Primitive religion is false, science true. But where for Tylor primitive religion, including myth, functions as the counterpart to scientific *theory*, for Frazer it functions even more as the counterpart to *applied* science, or technology. Where for Tylor primitive religion serves to *explain* events in the physical world, for Frazer it serves even more to *effect* events, above all the growth of crops. Where Tylor treats myth as an autonomous text, Frazer ties myth to ritual, which enacts it.

Frazer takes the myth of Adonis as one of the main examples, for him, of the chief myth in all mythologies: that of the god of vegetation. For Frazer, the myth of Adonis would have been acted out, and that ritualistic enactment would have been believed to work magically to effect whatever had been acted out. To have acted act out the resurfacing of Adonis would have been to effect it and in turn the resurfacing of the crops. The myth would have served not simply to explain why the crops had died—they had died because Adonis, in descending to the land of the dead, had died—but actually to revive the crops. For Frazer, the payoff of myth can scarcely be more practical: avoiding starvation. Frazer's interpretation of Adonis will be considered in detail in Chapter 4.

The biggest difficulty for Tylor's and Frazer's view of myth as the primitive counterpart to science is that it conspicuously fails to account for the retention of myth in the wake of science. If myth functions to do no more than science, why is it still around? Of course, Tylor and Frazer could promptly reply that whatever remains is not myth, and exactly because it is not serving a scientific-like function.

Yet neither Tylor nor Frazer can explain why myth, or religion as a whole, is still invoked *alongside* science to explain physical events. For example, whenever a handful of passengers survives a plane crash, the crash itself gets explained scientifically, but the survival often gets credited to intervention by God and not to, say, the location of the seats. Tylor and Frazer would doubtless reply that the survivors have simply not faced up to the incompatibility of their religious explanation with a scientific one. But why not argue instead that any appeal to consistency is outweighed by some more pressing need that for survivors a religious explanation alone can fulfil?

Lucien Lévy-Bruhl

Reacting against the views of Tylor, Frazer, and other members of what he imprecisely calls 'the English school of anthropology', the French philosopher and armchair anthropologist Lucien Lévy-Bruhl (1857–1939) insisted on a much wider divide between myth and science. Where for Tylor and Frazer primitives think like moderns, just less rigorously, for Lévy-Bruhl primitives think differently from moderns. Where for Tylor and Frazer primitive thinking is logical, just erroneous, for Lévy-Bruhl primitive thinking is plainly non-logical—or, in his preferred term, 'prelogical'.

According to Lévy-Bruhl, primitives believe not, as for Tylor, that all natural phenomena possess individual, human-like souls, or gods, but that all phenomena, including humans and their artefacts, are part of an impersonal sacred, or 'mystic', realm pervading the natural one. Primitives believe, further, that the 'participation' of all things in this mystic reality enables phenomena not only to affect one another magically but also to become one another, yet remain what they are: 'objects, beings, phenomena can be, though in a way incomprehensible to us [moderns], both themselves and something other than themselves'. The Bororo of Brazil declare themselves red araras, or parakeets, yet still human beings. Lévy-Bruhl calls this belief prelogical because it violates the law of non-contradiction: the notion that something can simultaneously be both itself and something else.

Where for Tylor and Frazer myth involves the same processes of observation, inference, and generalization as science, or at least of science in their inductivist view of it, for Lévy-Bruhl mythic thinking is the opposite of scientific thinking. Where for Tylor and Frazer primitives *perceive* the same world as moderns but simply *conceive* of it differently, for Lévy-Bruhl primitives see and in turn conceptualize the world differently from moderns—namely, as identical with themselves.

For Lévy-Bruhl, as for Tylor and Frazer, myth is part of religion, religion is primitive, and moderns have science rather than religion. But where Tylor in particular subsumes both religion and science under philosophy, Lévy-Bruhl associates philosophy with thinking freed from mystical identification with the world. Primitive thinking is non-philosophical because it is not detached from the world. Primitives have a whole mentality of their own, one evinced in their myths.

Even the use to which myth is put is for Lévy-Bruhl one of emotional involvement rather than, as for Tylor and Frazer, one of intellectual detachment. Primitives use religion, especially myth, not to explain or to control the world but instead to commune with it—more precisely, to restore the 'mystic' communion that has gradually begun to fade:

> Can myths then likewise be the products of primitive mentality which appear when this mentality is endeavouring to realize a participation no longer felt?

Presented with the myth of Adonis, Lévy-Bruhl would surely focus on Adonis' mystic relationship to the world. Ovid's Adonis is oblivious to all warnings about the dangers of the world because he imagines himself at home in the world, and at home because one with the world. He is unable to resist the goddesses because he sees them as his mother, with whom he seeks not intercourse but womb-like absorption. Between him and the goddesses there exists the primordial state of oneness that Lévy-Bruhl calls *participation mystique*.

Bronislaw Malinowski

One reaction to Lévy-Bruhl was to reassert the philosophical nature of myth—a reaction to be considered in Chapter 2. The key theorists here were Paul Radin and Ernst Cassirer. Another reaction was to accept Lévy-Bruhl's separation of myth from philosophy but not his characterization of myth as pre-philosophical or pre-scientific. The key figure here was the Polish-born anthropologist Bronislaw Malinowski (1884–1942), who early on moved to England. Where Lévy-Bruhl asserts that primitives seek to commune with nature rather than to explain it, Malinowski, like Frazer, asserts that primitives seek to control nature rather than to explain it. Both associate a philosophical approach with an explanatory, or intellectualist, one, and both associate that view with the British—for Malinowski, with Tylor but not also with Frazer. Both attribute this contrived notion of myth and, in general, of religion to a contrived notion of primitives.

Invoking Frazer, for whom myth and religion are the primitive counterpart to applied science, Malinowski argues that primitives are too busy scurrying to survive in the world to have the luxury of reflecting on it. Where for Frazer primitives use myth *in place of* science, which, again, is exclusively modern, for Malinowski primitives use myth as a *fallback* to science. Primitives possess not just the counterpart to science but science itself:

> [T]here is no doubt that even the lowest savage communities have the beginnings of science, however rudimentary.

Primitives use science to control the physical world. Where science stops, they turn to magic.

Where magic stops, primitives turn to myth—not to secure further control over the world, as Frazer would assume, but the opposite: to reconcile themselves to aspects of the world that cannot be controlled, such as natural catastrophes, illness, ageing, and death. Myths, which are not limited to religion, root these woes in the irreversible, primordial actions of either gods or humans. According to a typical myth, humans age because two forebears did something foolish that introduced old age irremediably into the world:

> The longed-for power of eternal youth and the faculty of rejuvenation which gives immunity from decay and age, have been lost by a small accident which it would have been in the power of a child and a woman to prevent.

Myth explains how, say, flooding arose—a god or a human brought it about—but primitive science and magic try to do something about it. By contrast, myth says that nothing can be done about it. Myths that serve to resign primitives to the uncontrollable are about physical phenomena. Myths about social phenomena, such as customs and laws, serve to persuade primitives to accept what *can* be resisted, as will be considered in Chapter 8.

What would Malinowski say of the myth of Adonis? He would likely concentrate on the myth as an expression of the ineluctability of death for all, would see Adonis as a human and not a god, and would take Adonis' obliviousness to his mortality as a lesson for others. But Malinowski's theory would truly work only if the myth *accounted for* mortality rather than presupposed it. Myth for Malinowski—and also, as we shall see, for Eliade—is about origins. Malinowski would be left with Ovid's version of the myth as an elongated account of the flower anemone, and Malinowski would have to show that the flower mattered to the lives of ancient Greeks or Romans. Like Tylor, he would take the myth literally.

Claude Lévi-Strauss

Reacting both against Malinowski's view of primitives as practical rather than intellectual and against Lévy-Bruhl's view of primitives as emotional rather than intellectual, the French structural anthropologist Claude Lévi-Strauss (1908–2009) boldly sought to revive an intellectualist view of primitives and of myth. At first glance Lévi-Strauss seems a sheer throwback to Tylor. For myth for Lévi-Strauss, just as for Tylor, is at once an exclusively primitive, yet nevertheless rigorously intellectual, enterprise. In declaring that 'the kind of logic which is used by mythical thought is as rigorous as that of modern science', Lévi-Strauss seems indistinguishable from Tylor.

Yet in fact Lévi-Strauss is severely critical of Tylor, for whom primitives create myth rather than science because they think less critically than moderns. For Lévi-Strauss, primitives create myth because they think differently from moderns—but, contrary to Lévy-Bruhl, still think and still think rigorously. For both Tylor and Lévi-Strauss, myth is the epitome of primitive thinking.

Where for Tylor primitive thinking is personalistic and modern thinking impersonal, for Lévi-Strauss primitive thinking is concrete and modern thinking abstract. Primitive thinking deals with phenomena qualitatively rather than, like modern thinking, quantitatively. It focuses on the observable, sensory aspects of phenomena rather than, like modern thinking, on the unobservable, non-sensory ones:

> For these men [i.e., primitives] ... the world is made up of minerals, plants, animals, noises, colors, textures, flavors, odors.... What separates the savage thought from [modern] scientific thought is perfectly clear—and it is not a greater or lesser thirst for logic. Myths manipulate those qualities of perception that modern thought, at the birth of modern science, exorcised from science.

Yet antithetically to Tylor, Lévi-Strauss considers myth no less scientific than modern science. Myth is simply part of the 'science of the concrete' rather than of the science of the abstract. Where for Tylor myth is the primitive counterpart to science per se, for Lévi-Strauss myth is the primitive counterpart to *modern* science. Myth *is* primitive science, but not thereby inferior science.

If myth is an instance of primitive thinking because it deals with concrete, tangible phenomena, it is an instance of thinking itself because it classifies phenomena, and into opposing categories. Lévi-Strauss maintains that all humans think in the form of pairs of oppositions and project them onto the world. Many cultural phenomena express these oppositions. Myth is distinctive in resolving or, more accurately, tempering the oppositions it expresses. Where for Tylor myth is like science precisely because it goes beyond observation to explanation, for Lévi-Strauss myth is outright scientific because it goes beyond the recording of observed contradictions to the tempering of them. Those contradictions are to be found not in the plot or myth but in what Lévi-Strauss famously calls the 'structure', and the approach to myth that is thereby called 'structuralist' will be accorded a chapter of its own, Chapter 7, in which the myth of Adonis will be analysed at length.

Karl Popper

Karl Popper (1902–94), the Viennese-born philosopher of science who eventually settled in England, breaks radically with Tylor. First, Tylor never explains how science ever emerged, since religion, including myth, provides a comprehensive and seemingly non-falsifiable explanation of all events in the physical world. Second, science for Tylor does not build on myth but simply replaces it. For Popper, science emerges *out of* myth: 'most of our scientific theories originate in myths'. Science originates not, however, out of the *acceptance* of myth but out of the *criticism* of it. By 'criticism' Popper means not rejection but assessment, which becomes scientific when it takes the form of subjection to attempts to falsify the truth claims made.

Going even further, Popper maintains that there are scientific as well as religious myths—this antithetically to Tylor, himself never cited by Popper. The difference between scientific and religious myths is not in their content but in the attitude towards them. Where religious myths are accepted dogmatically, scientific myths are questioned:

> My thesis is that what we call 'science' is differentiated from the older myths not by being something distinct from a myth, but by being accompanied by a second-order tradition—that of critically discussing the myth. We shall understand that, in a certain sense, science is myth-making just as religion is.

Popper even maintains that scientific theories *remain* myth-like, for theories, like myths, can never be proved, only disproved, and therefore remain uncertain. Still, scientific myth is testable. Myth without science is not.

It is not clear what Popper would be able to say of the myth of Adonis. The myths that grab him are creation myths, for they make bold conjectures about the origin of the world and thereby start the process of scientific theorizing. For the proverbial record the same Popper wrote a book entitled *The Myth of the Framework* and by 'myth' there means what William Rubinstein means in *The Myth of Rescue*: a staunchly held false conviction, one not to be further tested but to be abandoned!

Like Popper, the English classical philosopher F. M. Cornford (1874–1943) argued that Greek science grew out of myth and religion, but he limits himself to the content and considers not at all the attitude. For Cornford, science perpetuates, albeit in secular form, religious and mythical beliefs. Cornford contends that Greek science only subsequently severed its ties to religion and became empirical science. Cornford later argued that Greek science never severed its ties to religion and never became empirical science.

Tylor himself does contrast the testability of science to the untestability of myth, but he never specifies the nature of the test:

> We are being trained to the facts of physical science, which we can test and test again, and we feel it a fall from this high level of proof when we turn our minds to the old records which elude such testing, and are even admitted on all hands to contain statements not to be relied on.

Yet Tylor must grant primitives some capacity for criticism, for how else to account for the eventual replacement of myth by science? Who save the last generation of primitives was present to create science, to substitute it for myth, and to forge modernity?

Chapter 2
Myth and philosophy

The relationship between myth and science overlaps with the relationship between myth and philosophy, so that many of the theorists considered in Chapter 1 could have been considered here instead. Yet there is an even greater array of positions held on the relationship between myth and philosophy: that myth is part of philosophy, that myth *is* philosophy, that philosophy is myth, that myth grows out of philosophy, that philosophy grows out of myth, that myth and philosophy are independent of each other but serve the same function, and that myth and philosophy are independent of each other and serve different functions.

Paul Radin

Recall that where Tylor and Frazer alike subsumed both myth and science under philosophy, Lévy-Bruhl, in reaction, set myth against both science and philosophy. For him, primitive identification with the world, as evinced in myth, is the opposite of the detachment from the world demanded by science and philosophy.

In turn, the most abrupt reaction to Lévy-Bruhl came from the Polish-born anthropologist Paul Radin (1883–1959), who arrived in America as an infant. The title of his key book, *Primitive Man as Philosopher*, is self-explanatory. Though oddly Radin never mentions Tylor here, he in effect revives Tylor's view, while at once qualifying and extending it. Radin grants that *most* primitives are far from philosophical but observes that few persons in any culture are philosophical. He distinguishes between the average person, the 'man of action', and the exceptional person, the 'thinker':

> The former [i.e., the man of action] is satisfied that the world exists and that things happen. Explanations are of secondary consequence. He is ready to accept the first one that comes to hand. At bottom it is a matter of utter indifference. He does, however, show a predilection for one type of explanation as opposed to another. He prefers an explanation in which the purely mechanical relation between a series of events is specifically stressed. His mental rhythm—if I may be permitted to use this term—is characterized by a demand for endless repetition of the same event or, at best, of events all of which are on the same general level....Now the rhythm of the thinker is quite different. The postulation of a mechanical relation between events does not suffice. He insists on a description couched either in terms of a gradual progress and evolution from one to many and from simple to complex, or on the postulation of a cause and effect relation.

Both 'types of temperament' are to be found in all cultures, and in the same proportion. If Lévy-Bruhl is therefore wrong to deny that any primitives are thinkers, Tylor is equally wrong to assume that, to varying degrees, all are. But those primitives whom Radin does deem thinkers have a philosophical prowess far keener than Tylor, who calls them 'savage philosophers', grants them. For Radin, primitive speculations, found most fully in myths, do more than account for events in the physical world. The most that is even accounted for in the myth of Adonis is the perfume myrrh (Apollodorus, Ovid) and the flower anemone (Ovid). Myths for Radin deal with metaphysical topics of all kinds, such as the ultimate omponents of reality. Contrary to Tylor, primitives, furthermore, are capable of rigorous criticism. Likely for Radin, as definitely for Popper, the capacity for criticism is the hallmark of thinking.

Ernst Cassirer

A far less dismissive reaction to Lévy-Bruhl came from the German-born philosopher Ernst Cassirer (1874–1945). For Cassirer, wholly following Lévy-Bruhl, mythic, or 'mythopoeic', thinking is primitive, is laden with emotion, is part of religion, and is the projection of mystical oneness onto the world. Yet Cassirer claims to be breaking sharply with Lévy-Bruhl in asserting that mythic thinking has its own brand of logic. In actuality, Lévy-Bruhl says the same and invents the term 'prelogical' exactly to avoid labelling mythic thinking 'illogical' or 'nonlogical'. Cassirer also claims to be breaking with Lévy-Bruhl in stressing the autonomy of myth as a form of knowledge—language, art, and science being the other main forms:

> And indeed there has been no lack of attempts to explain myth
> by reducing it to another form of cultural life, whether knowledge
> [i.e. science], art, or language.

Yet Cassirer simultaneously maintains, no differently from Lévy-Bruhl, that myth is incompatible with science and that science succeeds it: 'Science arrives at its own form only by rejecting all mythical and metaphysical ingredients'. For both Cassirer and Lévy-Bruhl, myth is exclusively primitive and science exclusively modern. Still, Cassirer's characterization of myth as a form of *knowledge*—as one of humanity's symbol-making, world-creating activities—puts myth in the same genus as science, which is not quite where Lévy-Bruhl would put it.

Rudolf Bultmann and Hans Jonas

As philosophical as the approach to myth of especially earlier Cassirer is, he never contends that myth *is* philosophy. The theorists who do so are the German theologian Rudolf Bultmann (1884–1976) and the German-born philosopher Hans Jonas (1903–93), who eventually settled in the United States. The two not only take the meaning of myth from philosophy—from early, existentialist Martin Heidegger—but also confine themselves to the issue of meaning. No doubt because they are not, like most theorists, social scientists, they are not concerned with either the origin or the function of myth. Like some armchair anthropologists, they treat myth as an autonomous text rather than as part of Christian or Gnostic religion. But unlike Tylor, they do not even speculate from their armchairs about how myth arose or worked. While they treat the mythologies they study—the New Testament for Bultmann, Gnosticism for Jonas—as philosophy, the mythologies are still part of religion and so will be considered more fully in Chapter 3, on myth and religion.

Albert Camus

A more popular example of the reduction of myth to philosophy is to be found in the celebrated interpretation of the Greek myth of Sisyphus by Albert Camus (1913–60), the French existentialist writer. Among the figures whom Odysseus encounters in Tartarus, the part of Hades reserved for those who have offended Zeus, is Sisyphus, whose eternal punishment is to have to push a huge stone up a steep hill, only for it to roll back down every time just as he nears the top (see Figure 2). As Odysseus describes the sight,

> Also I saw Sisyphos. He was suffering strong pains, and with both arms embracing the monstrous stone, struggling with hands and feet alike, he would try to push the stone upward to the crest of the hill, but when it was on the point of going over the top, the force of gravity turned it backward, and the pitiless stone rolled back down to the level. He then tried once more to push it up, straining hard, and sweat ran all down his body, and over his head a cloud of dust rose.

(Homer, *The Odyssey*, Book XI, lines 593–600)

Homer does not disclose what Sisyphus' misdeed was, and ancient authorities differ. Still, for all ancients, Sisyphus was to be pitied. For Camus, he is to be admired. Rather than embodying the fate that awaits those few human beings who dare to defy the gods, Sisyphus symbolizes the fate of all humans, who find themselves

SISYPHE CONDAMNÉ À ROULER UNE PIERRE SUR LE HAUT D'UNE MONTAGNE, D'OÙ ELLE RETOMBE À L'INSTANT.
Sisyphus's Stone.

2. **Sisyphus in Tartarus, 18th-century engraving by B. Picart.**

condemned to live in a world without gods. He is admirable because he accepts the absurdity of human existence, which is less unfair than pointless. Instead of giving up and committing suicide, he toils on, even while fully aware that his every attempt will prove futile. He, not Odysseus, is the true hero, and his is the only kind of heroism that a meaningless, because godless, world allows. Camus uses the myth of Sisyphus to dramatize the human condition.

The myth of Sisyphus was no less a part of a religion than the myths analysed by Bultmann and Jonas were—and for Bultmann still are. But Camus, just like Bultmann and Jonas, treats myth as a sheer text, severed from any practising, institutionalized religion. For all three, myth is a philosophical tale, for, after all, myth for them *is* philosophy.

Chapter 3
Myth and religion

To approach myth from the field of religious studies is naturally to subsume myth under religion but is thereby to expose myth to the challenge to religion from science. Twentieth-century theories from religious studies have sought to reconcile myth with science by reconciling religion with science.

There have been two main strategies for reconciling the two. One tactic has been to re-characterize the subject matter of religion and therefore of myth. Religion, it has been argued, is not about the physical world, in which case religion is safe from any encroachment by science. The myths considered under this approach to religion are traditional myths, such as biblical and classical ones, but they are now read symbolically rather than literally. Myth, it is claimed, has been taken to be at odds with science because it has been misread. Tylor's tirade against those who take myth other than literally epitomizes this misreading of myth—by Tylor himself!

The other tactic has been to elevate seemingly secular phenomena to religious ones. As part of this elevation, myth is no longer confined to explicitly religious ancient stories. There are now overtly secular modern myths as well. For example, stories about heroes are at face value about mere human beings, but humans raised so high above ordinary mortals as to become virtual gods.

At the same time the actions of these 'gods' are not supernatural and are thus not incompatible with science. This approach retains a literal reading of myth but re-categorizes the literal status of the agents in myth.

There is a third tactic: replacing religious myths with secular ones. This strategy saves myth from the fate of religion by severing myth from religion. It is thus the opposite of the second tactic: turning secular myths into religious ones. The classic example of this tactic is Camus' interpretation of the myth of Sisyphus not as the punishment of a defiant human by the gods but as life in a world without gods. In uncoupling myth from religion, this tactic conspicuously falls outside the present chapter.

Rudolf Bultmann

The grandest exponents of a symbolic rendition of traditional religious myths have been Rudolf Bultmann and Hans Jonas, both discussed briefly in Chapter 2. As noted, the two confine themselves to their specialties, Christianity and Gnosticism, but nevertheless apply to them a theory of myth per se.

Taken literally, myth for Bultmann is exactly what it is for Tylor: a primitive explanation of the world, an explanation incompatible with a scientific one, and an explanation therefore unacceptable to moderns, who by definition accept science. Read literally, myth for Bultmann should be rejected as uncompromisingly as Tylor rejects it. But unlike Tylor, Bultmann reads myth symbolically. In his celebrated, if excruciatingly confusing, phrase, he 'demythologizes' myth, which means not eliminating, or 'demythicizing', the mythology but on the contrary preserving the mythology by extricating its true, symbolic meaning. To seek evidence of an actual worldwide flood, while dismissing the miraculous notion of an ark harbouring all species, would be to *demythicize* the Noah myth. To interpret the flood as a symbolic

statement about the precariousness of human life would be to
demythologize the myth.

Demythologized, myth ceases to be about the world and turns out
to be about the human *experience* of the world. Demythologized,
myth ceases to be an explanation at all and becomes an expression,
an expression of what it 'feels' like to live in the world. Myth
ceases to be merely primitive and becomes universal. It ceases
to be false and becomes true. It depicts the human condition.
In Bultmann's words,

> The real purpose of myth is not to present an objective picture of
> the world as it is, but to express man's understanding of himself in
> the world in which he lives. Myth should be interpreted not
> cosmologically, but anthropologically, or better still, existentially.

Taken literally, the New Testament in particular describes a
cosmic battle between good and evil beings for control of the
physical world. These supernatural figures intervene not only in
the operation of nature, as for Tylor, but also in the lives of human
beings. The beneficent beings direct humans to do good; the
malevolent ones compel them to do evil. Taken literally, the New
Testament describes a pre-scientific outlook.

Demythologized, the New Testament still refers in part to
the physical world, but now to a world ruled by a single,
non-anthropomorphic, transcendent God, who does not look
like a human being and who does not intervene miraculously in
the world. God still exists, but Satan becomes a mere symbol
of the evil inclinations within humans. Damnation refers not to
a future place but to one's present state of mind, which exists as
long as one rejects God. Salvation refers to one's state of mind
once one accepts God. There is no physical hell. Hell symbolizes
despair over the absence of God. Heaven refers not to a place in
the sky but to joy in the presence of God. The Kingdom comes

not outwardly, with cosmic upheavals, but inwardly, whenever one embraces God.

Overall, the New Testament, when demythologized, presents the opposing ways in which the world is experienced: the alienation from the world felt by those who have not yet found God versus the at-homeness in the world felt by those who have found God. For those without God, the world is cold, callous, and scary. For those with God, the world is warm, inviting, and safe.

Taken literally, myth, as a personalistic explanation of the physical world, is incompatible with science and is therefore unacceptable to moderns:

> Man's knowledge and mastery of the world have advanced to such an extent through science and technology that it is no longer possible for anyone seriously to hold the New Testament view of the world—in fact, there is no one who does.

Once demythologized myth is compatible with science because it now refers at once to the transcendent, non-physical world—as modern religion *without* myth does for Tylor—and, even more, to humans' experience of the physical one.

Bultmann's justification for translating the New Testament into existentialist terms is not, however, that otherwise moderns could not accept it. That argument would make truth subject to the times. Instead, the justification is that the true meaning of the New Testament has always been existential.

Yet to say that myth is acceptable to scientifically minded moderns is not to say why it should be accepted. In providing an existentialist *subject matter* of myth, Bultmann provides no existentialist *function*. Perhaps for him the function is self-evident: describing the human condition. But why bother describing that condition, and why use myth to do so? Bultmann cannot contend that myth *discloses* the human condition, for he himself enlists Heidegger's philosophy to find that meaning in myth.

As eager as Bultmann is to make myth acceptable to scientifically minded moderns, he is not prepared to interpret away—to demythicize—God altogether, and he has thereby been criticized for stopping short. Bultmann is a religious existentialist rather than, like Camus, an atheistic one.

What would Bultmann say of the myth of Adonis? Surely he would contrast the worlds in which Adonis finds himself. Adonis, never out of the hovering presence of a smothering goddess, is nurtured in a womb-like world, one wholly safe and sheltering. So immersed in it is he that the dangers from the 'real' world which, in Ovid's version, Venus desperately tries to impress on him simply do not register. Demythologized, the myth describes opposing experiences of the world—here not secular versus religious but infantile versus adult.

For the record, Bultmann is in fact inconsistent. Despite his seeming characterization of myth per se as a symbolic expression of the human condition, he takes literally the ancient mythologies out of which Christianity arose: those of Jewish apocalyptic and of Gnosticism. Bultmann thus restricts demythologization to Christianity. Yet with further inconsistency he acknowledges his debt to fellow existentialist Jonas' pioneering demythologization of Gnosticism!

Hans Jonas

Hans Jonas argues that ancient Gnosticism presents the same view of the human condition as modern existentialism. Both stress the radical alienation of human beings from the world:

> the essence of existentialism is a certain dualism, an estrangement between man and the world...There is [only] one situation...where

that condition has been realized and lived out with all the vehemence of a cataclysmic event. That is the gnostic movement.

But unlike Bultmann, who strives to bridge the gap between Christianity and modernity, Jonas acknowledges the divide between Gnosticism and modernity. He is therefore not seeking to placate modern Gnostics. There are none. Because ancient Gnosticism, unlike mainstream Christianity, sets immateriality against matter, humans remain alienated from the physical world even after they have found the true God. In fact, that god can be found only by rejecting the physical world and its false god. Gnostics overcome alienation from this world only by transcending it. But then for Gnostics estrangement is only temporary, whereas for moderns it is permanent. And where Gnostics were religious, moderns are atheistic.

Yet for Jonas, Gnostic mythology can still speak to moderns, and not just to modern believers, as for Bultmann, but also to modern sceptics. The mythology can do so because, rightly grasped, it addresses not the nature of the world but the nature of the experience of the world—that is, of this world. Jonas does not, like Camus, translate a world of gods into a world without them. Rather, he bypasses the religious nature of the Gnostic world. The *fact* of human alienation from the world, not the source of it or the solution to it, is the demythologized subject of myth for Jonas. Ignored therefore are Gnostic descriptions of the godhead, the emanations, the creator god, and the material world. No less ignored is the Gnostic prospect of escape from the material world. In short, the bulk of Gnostic mythology is reduced to mere mythology—to be discarded, or demythicized, just like *all* of mythology for Tylor. Bultmann, by contrast, retains God above all.

No more than Bultmann does Jonas offer any function of myth for moderns. Even if myth serves to express the human condition, why is it necessary to express that condition at all, let alone through myth, and again when existentialist philosophy already does so? Jonas does not say. Both he and Bultmann limit themselves to the meaning, or subject matter, of myth.

Bultmann's and Jonas' approach to myth could scarcely be more opposed to Tylor's. Tylor takes for granted that to be taken seriously, myth must be taken literally. For him, those who read myth symbolically trivialize it. Bultmann and Jonas, as well as such other theorists as Joseph Campbell, argue the opposite: that myth must be taken symbolically to be taken seriously. Where Tylor argues that myth is credible to primitives only because they take it literally, Bultmann and Jonas argue that myth was most credible to early Christians and ancient Gnostics because they took it existentially. Where Tylor argues that myth is incredible to moderns precisely because they rightly take it literally, Bultmann and Jonas argue that myth is credible to moderns only in so far as they rightly take it symbolically. Yet Tylor truly objects not to those theorists who read myth symbolically for moderns but to those who read it symbolically for primitives. He would thus berate Bultmann and Jonas far more for what they say of early Christians and ancient Gnostics than for what they say of moderns.

Ironically, Tylor, Bultmann, and Jonas all write in defence of myth. The difference is that for Tylor the defence demands the abandonment of myth in the wake of science, whereas for Bultmann and Jonas the defence requires the explication of the true meaning of myth in the wake of science. That meaning is not a new one concocted by moderns to save myth. It is the meaning that myth has always had but that, until pressed by the threat from science, has not been fully recognized. By forcing moderns to go back to the hoary text to discover what it has really been saying all along, science has turned a necessity into a virtue.

Mircea Eliade

Hagiographical biographies of celebrated figures transform them into near-gods and their sagas into myths. For example, immediately after the first Gulf War, biographies of the American supreme commander, 'Stormin Norman' Schwarzkopf, touted him as the smartest and bravest soldier in the world—so much smarter and braver than anyone else as to make him almost more than human.

The key theorist here is the Romanian-born historian of religions Mircea Eliade (1907–86), who spent the last three decades of his life in the United States. Unlike Bultmann—Jonas is less concerned with the issue—Eliade does not seek to reconcile myth with science by interpreting myth symbolically. He reads myth as literally as Tylor does. And for him, as much as for Tylor, myth is an explanation, though, strictly, of the origin of a phenomenon rather than of its recurrence. Unlike Bultmann and Jonas, Eliade does not try to update traditional myths. But rather than, like Tylor, sticking to traditional, explicitly religious myths, he turns to modern, seemingly non-religious ones. Still, he does not try to reconcile those myths with science, as Bultmann and Jonas would. Instead, he appeals to the sheer presence of them to argue for their compatibility with science: if moderns, who for Eliade no less than for the others are scientific by definition, also have myth, then myth simply must be compatible with science.

Eliade's criterion for myth is that a story attribute to its subject a feat so exceptional as to turn its subject into a superhuman figure. Myth describes how, in primaeval, 'sacred' time, a god or near-god created a phenomenon that continues to exist. That phenomenon can be social *or* natural—for example, marriage or rain:

> myth tells how, through the deeds of Supernatural Beings, a reality came into existence, be it the whole of reality, the Cosmos, or only a fragment of reality—an island, a species of plant, a particular kind of human behavior, an institution.

Where only outright gods are credited with creating natural phenomena, 'culture heroes' are credited with creating social phenomena. In both cases the mythic feat is creation. For Tylor, the feat is recurrence.

Yet myth does more than explain, which turns out to be a mere means to an end. The end is regeneration. To hear, to read, and especially to re-enact a myth is magically to return to the time when the myth took place, the time of the origin of whatever phenomenon it explains:

> But since ritual recitation of the cosmogonic myth implies reactualization of that primordial event, it follows that he for whom it is recited is magically projected *in illo tempore*, into the 'beginning of the World'; he becomes contemporary with the cosmogony.

Myth works like a magic carpet, albeit one that goes in a single direction. In returning one to primordial time, myth reunites one with the gods, for it is then when they are believed to be nearest, as the biblical case of 'the Lord God['s] walking in the garden in the cool of the day' typifies (Genesis 3.8). That 'reunion' reverses the post-Edenic separation from the gods and renews one spiritually. The ultimate payoff of myth is experiential: encountering divinity. No theory of myth could be more rooted in religion than Eliade's.

Clearly, science offers no regenerative function. Science simply explains. Myth, then, can do things that science cannot. Yet Eliade's main argument for the survival of myth is not that it serves a unique function but that it serves that function for moderns as well as for primitives. According to Eliade, moderns fancy themselves scrupulously rational, intellectual, unsentimental, and forward-looking—in short, scientific. Yet even they, maintains Eliade, cannot dispense with myth:

A whole volume could well be written on the myths of modern man, on the mythologies camouflaged in the plays that he enjoys, in the books that he reads. The cinema, that 'dream factory', takes over and employs countless mythical motifs....Even reading includes a mythological function...because, through reading, the modern man succeeds in obtaining an 'escape from time' comparable to the 'emergence from time' effected by myths.

Plays, books, and films are like myths because they reveal the existence of another, often earlier world alongside the everyday one—a world of extraordinary figures and events akin to those found in traditional myths. Furthermore, the actions of those figures account for the present state of the everyday world. Most of all, moderns get so absorbed in plays, books, and films that they imagine themselves back in the time of myth. Where Bultmann and Jonas contend meekly that moderns *can* have myth, Eliade declares boldly that they *do*. If even avowed atheists have myth, then surely myth is not merely acceptable to moderns, as for Bultmann and Jonas, but ineluctable. It is pan-human. Where Tylor and Frazer assume that myth is the victim of the process of secularization, Eliade argues that no real secularization has occurred. Religion and, with it, myth remain, just 'camouflaged'.

How to apply Eliade to the case of Adonis, who seems as far from heroic as can be? Like the other Greek antiheroes Icarus and Phaëthon, Adonis imagines himself omnipotent. In actuality, he, like them, is oblivious to the dangers of the world and dies as a result of his narcissistic foolhardiness.

A modern Adonis would be John F. Kennedy, Jr (1960–99; see Figure 3), a beckoning hero to many and an irresistible sex symbol to women. Ignoring Venus-like warnings, he died when he recklessly insisted on flying in weather conditions for which a mere novice like him was in fact egregiously unprepared. In his

3. J. F. Kennedy, Jr on the cover of *US Weekly*, June 2000.

plunge to earth he was even more like Icarus and Phaëthon. The widespread mourning for J. F. K., Jr, was for a would-be hero rather than for an accomplished one.

A more suitable figure for Eliade would be the indisputable hero George Washington (1732–99). Revered by all Americans as the father of the country, Washington first served as Commander in Chief of the Continental Army in the war against the British, who were finally defeated in 1781 (see Figure 4). He then retired from public life but returned to preside over the Constitutional

4. *Washington before Yorktown* **by Rembrandt Peale.**

Convention, where his support was considered indispensable for the ratification of the Constitution. Washington was unanimously elected the first President of the United States (by the Electoral College) in 1789, was then unanimously re-elected, and would have been re-elected anew had he been willing to serve. He was held in such awe that many revolutionaries feared that he or his supporters would establish a monarchy and thereby undo the republican goals for which the Revolution had been fought. His resistance to this temptation made him even more revered.

The reverence accorded Washington by Americans in his time and long afterwards bordered on deification, and the treatment of him constituted virtual worship. Even before he became the first President, let alone while and after he served, there were coins bearing his image, an unprecedented number of paintings and sculptures of him, songs and poems praising him, counties and towns named after him, elaborate celebrations of his birthdays, and tumultuous receptions for him wherever he went. From the bestselling hagiographical biography by Mason Weems comes the most famous story about Washington: that the scrupulously honest young George could not lie when asked who had cut down his father's cherry tree. For Eliade, a myth honours its subject's establishing something in the physical or social world that continues to this day—here America itself. A historian's description of the birthday celebrations during Washington's presidency captures the 'cult' of Washington:

> [T]he observance of Washington's Birthday took on the character of a religious rite....Washington's Birthday was indeed a sacred day: a time for communion, a time when the sanctity of the nation, and the strength of the people's attachment to it, could be reaffirmed.

Long after his death, the celebration of Washington's birthday, which even today remains a national holiday, served not merely to commemorate his deeds but to bring them, and him, alive. Part of the celebration—the ritual—was the recitation of the highpoints of his biography—the myth. The bandied American line 'George Washington slept here' evinces the ultimate function of myth of Eliade: providing contact with a deity.

Of course, a sceptic can demur. Does the celebration of a dead hero's deeds really bring the hero back to life? Do celebrants really believe that they have travelled back in reality and not merely in their imagination? And in so far as the social sciences explain the lasting accomplishments of heroes, what is left for myth to explain? As affecting as Eliade's effort to secure a firm place for myth in the modern, scientific world is, is it convincing?

Chapter 4
Myth and ritual

Myth is commonly taken to be words, often in the form of a story. A myth is read or heard. It says something. Yet there is an approach to myth that deems this view of myth artificial. According to the myth and ritual, or myth-ritualist, theory, myth does not stand by itself but is tied to ritual. Myth is not just a statement but an action. The least compromising form of the theory maintains that all myths have accompanying rituals and all rituals accompanying myths. In tamer versions some myths may flourish without rituals and some rituals without myths. Alternatively, myths and rituals may originally operate together but subsequently go their separate ways. Or myths and rituals may arise separately but subsequently coalesce. Whatever the tie between myth and ritual, the myth-ritualist theory differs from other theories of myth and from other theories of ritual in focusing on the tie.

William Robertson Smith

The myth-ritualist theory was pioneered by the Scottish biblicist and Arabist William Robertson Smith (1846–94). In his *Lectures on the Religion of the Semites* Smith argued that belief is central to *modern* religion but not to *ancient* religion, in which ritual was central. Smith grants that ancients doubtless performed rituals only for some reason. But the reason was insignificant and could even fluctuate. And rather than a formal declaration of belief, or a creed, the reason was a story, or a *myth*, which simply described 'the circumstances under which the rite first came to be established, by the command or by the direct example of the god'. Myth was 'secondary'. Where ritual was obligatory, myth was optional. Where ritual was set, any myth would do. And myth did not even arise until the original, non-mythic reason given for the ritual had somehow been forgotten.

While Smith was the first to argue that myths must be understood vis-à-vis rituals, the nexus by no means requires that myths and rituals be of equal importance. For Smith, there would never have been myth without ritual, whether or not without myth there would have ceased to be ritual.

Because Adonis was a Semitic god, Smith includes him in his *Lectures*. As part of his overall argument that ancient religion had no sense of sin, he contrasts the death of Adonis, the god of vegetation, to that of Christ:

> The Canaanite Adonis or Tammuz…was regarded by his worshippers as the source of all natural growth and fertility. His death therefore meant a temporary suspension of the life of nature…And this death of the life of nature the worshippers lament out of natural sympathy, without any moral idea, just as modern man is touched with melancholy at the falling of the autumn leaves.

Originally, there was just the ritualistic sacrifice to the god Adonis, a sacrifice made for some non-mythic reason. Once that reason was forgotten, the myth of Adonis as the dying and rising god of vegetation was created to account for the ritual. As pagan rather than Christian, the myth deemed the death lamentable but not sinful.

One major limitation of Smith's theory is that it explains only myth and not ritual, which is simply presupposed. Another limitation is that the theory obviously restricts myth to ritual, though Smith does trace the subsequent development of myth independent of ritual.

E. B. Tylor

In claiming that myth is an explanation of ritual, Smith was denying the standard conception of myth, espoused classically by E. B. Tylor. According to Tylor, myth is an explanation of the physical world and not of anything social, such as ritual. Myth operates independently of ritual. Myth is a statement, not an action, and amounts to creed, merely presented in the form of a story. For Tylor, ritual is to myth as, for Smith, myth is to ritual: secondary. Where for Smith myth presupposes ritual, for Tylor ritual presupposes myth. For Tylor, myth functions to explain the world as an end in itself. Ritual at most applies that explanation to control the world. Ritual is the *application*, not the *subject*, of myth. The subject remains the world. Both because ritual depends on myth and, even more, because explanation is for Tylor more important than control, myth is a more important aspect of religion than ritual.

Smith is like Tylor in one key respect. For both, myth is wholly ancient. Modern religion is without myth—and without ritual as well. Myth and ritual are not merely ancient but *primitive*. In fact, for both Tylor and Smith, ancient religion is but a case of primitive religion, which is the fundamental foil to modern religion. Where for Tylor modern religion is without myth and ritual because it is no longer about the physical world and is instead a combination of ethics and metaphysics, for Smith modern religion is without myth and ritual because it is a combination of ethics and creed. For Tylor, modern religion, because bereft of myth, is a come-down from its ancient and primitive height. For Smith, modern religion, because severed from myth and, even more, from ritual, is a leap beyond its ancient and primitive beginnings. The epitome of modern religion for Smith is his own vigorously anti-ritualistic, because anti-Catholic, Presbyterianism.

J. G. Frazer

In the several editions of *The Golden Bough* J. G. Frazer developed the myth-ritualist theory far beyond that of his friend Smith, to whom he dedicates the work. While *The Golden Bough* is best known for its tripartite division of all culture into the stages of magic, religion, and science, the bulk of the tome in fact concerns an intermediate stage between religion and science—a stage of magic and religion combined. Only in this in-between stage, itself still ancient and primitive, is myth-ritualism to be found, for only here do myths and rituals work together.

Frazer, rarely consistent, actually presents two distinct versions of the myth-ritualism of this in-between stage. In the first version, the one already discussed in Chapter 1, myth describes the life of the god of vegetation, the chief god of the pantheon, and ritual enacts the myth describing his death and rebirth. The ritual operates on the basis of the magical Law of Similarity, according to which the imitation of an action causes it to happen. The clearest example of this brand of magic is voodoo. The ritual directly manipulates the god of vegetation, not vegetation itself, but as the god goes, so automatically goes vegetation. That vegetation is under the direct control of a god is the legacy of religion. That vegetation can be controlled, even if only indirectly through the god, is the legacy of magic. The combination of myth and ritual is the combination of religion and magic:

> Thus the old magical theory of the seasons was displaced, or rather supplemented, by a religious theory. For although men now attributed the annual cycle of change primarily to corresponding changes in their deities, they still thought that by performing certain magical rites they could aid the god who was the principle of life, in his struggle with the opposing principle of death. They imagined that they could recruit his failing energies and even raise him from the dead.

The ritual is performed whenever one wants winter to end, presumably when stored-up provisions are running low (see Figure 5). A human being, often the king, plays the role of the god and acts out what he thereby magically induces the god to do.

In Frazer's second, till now unmentioned, version of myth-ritualism the king is central. Here the king does not merely act the part of the god but is himself divine, by which Frazer means that the god resides in him. Just as the health of vegetation depends on the health of its god, so now the health of the god depends on the health of the king: as the king goes, so goes the god of vegetation, and so in turn goes vegetation itself. To ensure a steady supply of food, the community kills its king while he is still in his prime and thereby safely transfers the soul of the god to his successor:

> For [primitives] believe...that the king's life or spirit is so sympathetically bound up with the prosperity of the whole country, that if he fell ill or grew senile the cattle would sicken and cease to multiply, the crops would rot in the fields, and men would perish of widespread disease. Hence, in their opinion, the only way of averting these calamities is to put the king to death while he is still hale and hearty, in order that the divine spirit which he has inherited from his predecessors may be transmitted in turn by him to his successor while it is still in full vigour and has not yet been impaired by the weakness of disease and old age.

The king is killed either at the end of a short term or at the first sign of infirmity. As in the first version, the aim is to end winter, which now is attributed to the weakening of the king. How winter can ever, let alone annually, come if the king is removed at or even before the onset of any debilitation, Frazer never explains.

In any event this second version of myth-ritualism has proved the more influential by far, even though it actually provides only a

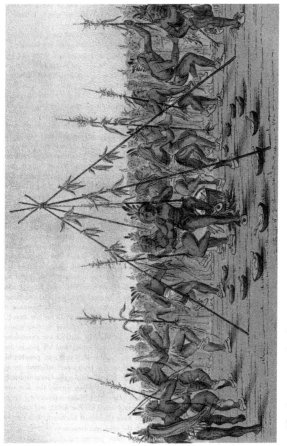

5. The Green Corn fertility dance of the Minatarees of North America, 19th-century illustration by George Catlin.

tenuous link between religious myth and magical ritual. Instead of enacting the myth of the god of vegetation, the ritual simply changes the residence of the god from the body of the incumbent king to that of his successor. The king dies not in imitation of the death of the god but as a sacrifice to preserve the health of the god. What part myth plays here, it is not easy to see. Instead of reviving the god by magical imitation, the ritual revives the god by a substitution.

In Frazer's first, truly myth-ritualist scenario myth arises prior to ritual rather than, as for Smith, after it. The myth that gets enacted in the combined stage emerges in the stage of religion and therefore antedates the ritual to which it is applied. In the combined stage myth, as for Smith, explains the point of ritual, but from the outset.

Myth gives ritual its original and sole meaning. Without the myth of the death and rebirth of that god, the death and rebirth of the god of vegetation would scarcely be ritualistically enacted. Still, myth for Frazer, as for Tylor, is an explanation of the world—of the course of vegetation—and not just, as for Smith, of ritual. But for Frazer, unlike Tylor, explanation is only a means to control, so that myth is the ancient and primitive counterpart to applied science rather than, as for Tylor, to scientific theory. Ritual may still be the application of myth, but myth is subordinate to ritual.

The severest limitation of Frazer's myth-ritualism is not only that it, like Smith's, precludes modern myths and rituals but also that it restricts even ancient and primitive myth-ritualism to myths about the god of vegetation, and really only to myths about the death and rebirth of that god.

Where Smith discusses the case of Adonis only in passing, Frazer makes Adonis a key example of the myth and ritual pattern of the dying and rising god of vegetation. Consistently or not,

Frazer actually places Adonis in all three of his pre-scientific stages of culture: those of magic, of religion, and of magic and religion combined.

Frazer locates the celebrated 'gardens' of Adonis in his first, magical stage. In this stage humans believe that impersonal forces rather than gods cause events in the physical world. Ancient Greeks would plant seeds in earth-filled pots placed on the roof, not to persuade a god to grant growth but, by the magical Law of Similarity, to force the impersonal earth itself to grow: 'For ignorant people suppose that by mimicking the effect which they desire to produce they actually help to produce it.' Because there are no gods in this stage, Adonis can hardly be a god of vegetation. Rather, he is vegetation itself. Vegetation does not symbolize Adonis; Adonis symbolizes vegetation.

In Frazer's second, religious stage gods replace magical laws as the source of events in the physical world, so that Adonis becomes, at least on the literal level, the god of vegetation. As the god of vegetation, Adonis could, most simply, have been asked for crops. Or the request could have been reinforced by obedience to the god's ritualistic and ethical dictates. Frazer himself writes that rites of mourning were performed for Adonis—not, as in the next stage, to undo his death but to seek his forgiveness for it. For Adonis has died not, as in the next stage, because he has descended to the Underworld but because in cutting, stamping, and grinding the corn—the specific part of vegetation he symbolizes—humans have killed him. Rather than 'the natural decay of vegetation in general under the summer heat or the winter cold', the death of Adonis is 'the violent destruction of the corn by man'. Yet Adonis is somehow still sufficiently alive to be capable of punishing humans, something that the rituals of forgiveness are intended to avert. Since, however, Adonis dies because vegetation itself does, the god is here really, as in the first stage, only a metaphor for the element that he supposedly controls. Again, as vegetation goes, so goes Adonis.

In Frazer's third, combined stage Adonis seems at last a god. If in stage two as vegetation goes, so goes Adonis, now as Adonis goes, so seemingly goes vegetation. Adonis' death means his descent to the Underworld for his stay with Persephone. Frazer assumes that whether or not Adonis has willed his descent, he is too weak to ascend by himself. By acting out his rebirth, humans facilitate it. On the one hand the enactment employs the magical Law of Similarity. On the other hand the enactment does not, as in the first stage, compel but only bolsters Adonis, who, despite his present state of death, is yet hearty enough to revive himself, just not unassisted. In this stage gods still control the physical world, but their effect on it is automatic rather than deliberate. To enact the rebirth of Adonis is to spur his rebirth and, through it, the rebirth of vegetation.

Yet even in this stage the sole aspect of Adonis' life considered by Frazer is that which parallels the annual course of vegetation: Adonis' death and rebirth. Adonis' otherwise *unnatural* life, beginning with his incestuous birth, is ignored. Ignored above all is Adonis' final death, the unnatural cause—killing, even murder—aside. And so Frazer must do. For if Adonis' life is to symbolize the course of vegetation, Adonis must continually die and be reborn. Yet he does not. By whatever means Adonis in Apollodorus' version overcomes death annually, he does not do so indefinitely. In Ovid's version Adonis has never before died and been reborn, and Venus is disconsolate exactly because he is gone once and for all. How, then, can his short, mortal life symbolize eternal rebirth, and how can he be a god? Frazer never reveals.

Finally, Frazer, once again oblivious to inconsistency, simultaneously declares Adonis' life in even the combined stage to be but a symbol of the course of vegetation itself: the myth that Adonis spent a portion of the year in the Underworld

is explained most simply and naturally by supposing that he represented vegetation, especially the corn, which lies buried in the earth half the year and reappears above ground the other half.

Adonis now proves to be not the cause of the fate of vegetation but only a metaphor for that fate, so that in stage three as well as in stage two as vegetation goes, so goes Adonis, and not vice versa. How myth-ritualism is possible when there is no longer a god to be ritualistically revived and when there is only a description, not an explanation, of the course of vegetation is not easy to see. In now taking mythology as a symbolic description of natural processes, Frazer is like a group of largely German 19th-century theorists known appropriately as nature mythologists.

Jane Harrison and S. H. Hooke

The next stage in the myth-ritualist theory came with Jane Harrison (1850–1928) and S. H. Hooke (1874–1968), the English leaders of the initial main groups of myth-ritualists: classicists and biblicists. Their positions are close. Both largely follow Frazer's first myth-ritualist scheme, though Hooke, nearly as inconsistent as Frazer, sometimes follows the second scheme. Unlike Frazer, Hooke and Harrison postulate no distinct, prior stages of magic and of religion. Both begin instead with the equivalent of Frazer's combined stage. Like Frazer, they deem myth-ritualism the ancient and primitive counterpart to modern science, which replaces not only myth-ritualism but myth and ritual per se. Harrison and Hooke follow Frazer most of all in their willingness to see heretofore elevated, superior religions—those of Hellenic Greece and of ancient Israel—as primitive. The conventional, pious view had been, and often continues to be, that Greece and Israel stood above the benighted magical endeavours of their neighbours.

Venturing beyond both Frazer and Hooke, Harrison adds to the ritual of the renewal of vegetation the ritual of initiation into society. She even argues that the original ritual, while still performed annually, was exclusively initiatory. There was no myth, so that for her, as for Smith, ritual precedes myth. God was only the projection of the euphoria produced by the ritual. Subsequently, god became the god of vegetation, the myth of the death and rebirth of that god arose, and the ritual of initiation became an agricultural ritual as well. Just as the initiates symbolically died and were reborn as full-fledged members of society, so the god of vegetation and in turn crops literally died and were reborn. In time, the initiatory side of the combined ritual faded, and only the Frazerian, agricultural ritual remained.

Both Harrison and Hooke go further than Frazer. For all three, myth provides the script for ritual. But where for Frazer the power of myth is merely dramatic, for Harrison and Hooke the spoken word is outright magical. Contemporary myth-ritualists like the American classicist Gregory Nagy appeal to the nature of oral, as opposed to written, literature to argue that myth was originally so closely tied to ritual, or performance, as to be ritualistic itself:

> Once we view myth as performance, we can see that myth itself is a form of ritual: rather than think of myth and ritual separately and only contrastively, we can see them as a continuum in which myth is a verbal aspect of ritual while ritual is a notional aspect of myth.

How this position goes beyond that of Hooke and Harrison is far from clear.

Application of the theory

The classicists Gilbert Murray, F. M. Cornford, and A. B. Cook, all English or English-resident, applied Harrison's theory to such ancient Greek phenomena as tragedy, comedy, the Olympic Games, science, and philosophy. These seemingly secular, even anti-religious phenomena are interpreted as latent expressions of the myth of the death and rebirth of the god of vegetation.

Among biblicists, the Swede Ivan Engnell, the Welshman Aubrey Johnson, and the Norwegian Sigmund Mowinckel differed over the extent to which ancient Israel in particular adhered to the myth-ritualist pattern. Engnell sees an even stronger adherence than the cautious Hooke; Johnson and especially Mowinckel, a weaker one.

Invoking Frazer, Bronislaw Malinowski, whose theory was considered in Chapter 1, applied his own, qualified version of the theory to the myths of native peoples worldwide. Malinowski argues that myth, which for him, as for Smith, explains the origin of ritual, gives rituals a hoary past and thereby sanctions them. Society depends on myth to spur adherence to rituals. But if all rituals depend on myth, so for Malinowski do many other cultural practices on which society depends. They have myths of their own. Myth and ritual are therefore not coextensive.

Mircea Eliade, whose theory was discussed in Chapter 3, applied a similar form of the theory, but he goes beyond Malinowski to apply the theory to modern as well as primitive cultures. Myth for him, too, sanctions phenomena of all kinds, not just rituals, by giving them a primaeval origin. For him, too, then, myth and ritual are not coextensive. But Eliade again goes beyond Malinowski in stressing the importance of the ritualistic enactment of myth in the fulfilment of the ultimate function of myth. When enacted, myth acts as a time machine, carrying one back to the time of the myth and thereby bringing one close to god.

Application of the theory to literature

The most notable application of the myth-ritualist theory outside of religion has been to literature. Harrison herself boldly derived all art, not just literature, from ritual. She speculates that gradually people ceased believing that the imitation of an action caused that action to occur. Yet rather than abandoning ritual, they now practised it as an end in itself. Ritual for its own sake became art, of which her clearest example is drama. More modestly than she, Murray and Cornford rooted specifically Greek epic, tragedy, and

comedy in myth-ritualism. Murray then extended the theory
to Shakespeare.

Other standard-bearers of the theory have included Jessie Weston
on the Grail legend, E. M. Butler on the Faust legend, C. L. Barber
on Shakespearean comedy, Herbert Weisinger on Shakespearean
tragedy and on tragedy per se, Francis Fergusson on tragedy, Lord
Raglan on hero myths and on literature as a whole, and Northrop
Frye and Stanley Edgar Hyman on literature generally. As literary
critics, these myth-ritualists have understandably been concerned
less with myth itself than with the mythic origin of literature. Works
of literature are interpreted as the outgrowth of myths once tied to
rituals. For those literary critics indebted to Frazer, as the majority
are, literature harks back to Frazer's second myth-ritualist scenario.
'The king must die' becomes the familiar summary line.

For literary myth-ritualists, myth becomes literature when myth is
severed from ritual. Myth tied to ritual is religious literature; myth
cut off from ritual is secular literature, or plain literature. When
tied to ritual, myth can serve any of the active functions ascribed
to it by myth-ritualists. Bereft of ritual, myth is reduced to mere
commentary.

Literary myth-ritualism is a theory not of myth and ritual
themselves, both of which are assumed, but of their impact on
literature. Yet it is not a theory of literature either, for it refuses
to reduce literature to myth. Literary myth-ritualism is an
explanation of the transformation of myth and ritual into
literature, and it will be considered in detail in Chapter 5.

René Girard

In *The Hero*, which will be discussed at length in Chapter 5, Lord
Raglan extends Frazer's second myth-ritualist scenario by turning
the king who dies for the community into a hero. In *Violence
and the Sacred* and many subsequent works, the French-born,

American-resident literary critic René Girard (b. 1923) offers an ironic twist to the theory of Raglan, himself never cited. Where Raglan's hero is willing to die for the community, Girard's hero is killed or exiled by the community for having caused their present woes. Indeed, the 'hero' is initially considered a criminal, who deserves to die. Only subsequently is the villain turned into a hero, who, as for Raglan, dies selflessly for the community. Both Raglan and Girard cite Oedipus as their fullest example. (Their doing so makes neither a Freudian. Both spurn Freud.) For Girard, the transformation of Oedipus from reviled exile in Sophocles' *Oedipus the King* to revered benefactor in Sophocles' *Oedipus at Colonus* typifies the transformation from criminal to hero.

Yet this change is for Girard only the second half of the process. The first half is the change from innocent victim to criminal. Originally, violence erupts in the community. The cause is the inclination, innate in human nature, to imitate others and thereby to desire the same objects as those of the imitated. Imitation leads to rivalry, which leads to violence. Desperate to end the violence, the community selects an innocent member to blame for the turmoil. This 'scapegoat' can be anyone and can range from the lowliest member of society to the highest, including, as with Oedipus, the king. The victim is usually killed, though, as with Oedipus, sometimes exiled. The killing is the ritualistic sacrifice. Rather than *directing* the ritual, as for Frazer, myth for Girard is created *after* the killing to *excuse* it. Myth comes from ritual, as for Smith, but it comes to *justify* rather than, as for Smith, to explain the ritual. Myth turns the scapegoat into a criminal, who deserved to die, and then turns the criminal into a hero, who has died voluntarily for the good of the community.

Girard's theory, which centres on the place of the protagonist in society, would seem hopelessly inapplicable to the myth of Adonis. Adonis hardly dies willingly or selflessly. The very worlds he inhabits—the woods and the Underworld—seem as far removed from society as can be. In Chapter 8 this myth will nevertheless be interpreted socially, and Girard's own interpretation of the myth of Oedipus will be presented.

While Girard never cites Raglan, he does regularly cite Frazer. Confining himself to Frazer's second myth-ritualist scenario, Girard lauds Frazer for recognizing the key primitive ritual of regicide but berates him for missing its real origin and function. For Frazer, sacrifice is the practical application of a benighted, pre-scientific explanation of the world: the king is killed and replaced so that the god of vegetation, whose soul resides in the incumbent, can either retain or regain his health. The function of the sacrifice is wholly agricultural. There is no hatred of the victim, who simply fulfils his duty as king and is celebrated throughout for his self-sacrifice. According to Girard, Frazer thereby falls for the mythic cover-up. The real origin and function of ritual and subsequent myth are social rather than agricultural, as will be discussed in Chapter 8.

Walter Burkert

Perhaps the first to temper the dogma that myths and rituals are inseparable was the American anthropologist Clyde Kluckhohn. The German classicist Walter Burkert (1931–2015) has gone well beyond Kluckhohn in not merely permitting but outright assuming the original independence of myth and ritual. He maintains that when the two do come together, they do not just serve a common function, as Kluckhohn assumes, but reinforce each other. Myth bolsters ritual by giving merely human behaviour a divine origin: do this because the gods did or do it. Conversely, ritual bolsters myth by turning a mere story into prescribed behaviour of the most dutiful kind: do this on pain of anxiety, if not punishment. Where for Smith myth serves ritual, for Burkert ritual equally serves myth.

Like Girard, Burkert roots myth in sacrifice and roots sacrifice in aggression, but he does not limit sacrifice to human sacrifice, and he roots sacrifice itself in hunting—the original expression of aggression (see Figure 6). Moreover, myth for Burkert functions not to hide the reality of sacrifice, as for Girard, but on the contrary to preserve it and thereby to retain its psychological and social effects. Finally, Burkert connects myths not only to rituals of sacrifice but also, like Harrison, to rituals of initiation. Myth here serves the same socializing function as ritual.

Ritual for Burkert is 'as if' behaviour. To take his central example, the 'ritual' is not actual hunting, with its own customs and formalities, but dramatized hunting. The function is no longer that of securing food, as for Frazer, for the ritual proper arises only after farming has supplanted hunting as the prime source of food:

6. **Hunting the Calydon Boar, Laconian Greek cup from Cerveteri, 6th century BC.**

Hunting lost its basic function with the emergence of agriculture some ten thousand years ago. But hunting ritual had become so important that it could not be given up.

The communal nature of actual hunting, and of ritualized hunting thereafter, functioned to assuage anxiety over one's own aggression and one's own mortality, and at the same time functioned to cement a bond among participants. The functions were psychological and sociological, not agricultural.

The myth of Adonis would present an ironic case for Burkert. Not only is Adonis' hunting solitary rather than communal, but Adonis is scarcely a real hunter, let alone one racked by anxiety. For him, hunting is more a sport than a life-and-death encounter. Therefore hunting can hardly abet him either psychologically or socially. Yet his saga can still function as a warning to others, as will be proposed in Chapter 8.

Chapter 5
Myth and literature

The relationship between myth and literature has taken varying forms. The most obvious form has been the use of myth in works of literature. A standard theme in literature courses has been the tracing of classical figures, events, and themes in Western literature thereafter—beginning with the Church Fathers, who utilized pagan mythology even while fighting paganism itself, and proceeding through Petrarch, Boccacio, Dante, Chaucer, Spenser, Shakespeare, Milton, Goethe, Byron, Keats, and Shelley, and then down to Joyce, Eliot, Gide, Cocteau, Anouilh, and Eugene O'Neill. The same has commonly been done for biblical myths. Both groups of myths have alternatively been read literally, been read symbolically, been rearranged, and been outright re-created. And they are to be found in all of the arts, including music and film. While not an artist, Freud used the figure Oedipus to name the most fundamental human drives. His rival C. G. Jung named the female counterpart after Electra. Freud took from psychiatrists the figure Narcissus to name self-love.

The pervasiveness of classical, or pagan, mythology is even more of a feat than that of biblical mythology, for classical mythology has survived the demise of the religion of which, two thousand years ago, it was a part. By contrast, biblical mythology has been sustained by the near-monolithic presence of the religion of which it remains a part. Indeed, classical mythology has been preserved by the culture tied to the religion that killed off classical religion. Till recently, the very term 'paganism' has had a negative connotation. That classical mythology has survived where the rest of its religion has not is an ironic reversal of Tylor's view of the differing fates of both, though Tylor is referring to the survival of Christianity, not of paganism, and to the survival of Christianity in the face of modern science, not of a rival religion.

Mythic themes in literature

Deeper than the perpetuation in literature of mythic figures, events, and categories has been the perpetuation of mythic themes. In 'On the Teaching of Modern Literature' (1961) Lionel Trilling, the most celebrated American literary critic of the 20th century, asserted that a theme in modern literature so central as 'to constitute one of the shaping and controlling ideas of our epoch' has been 'the disenchantment of our culture with culture itself'. He contends that 'the characteristic element of modern literature … is the bitter line of hostility to civilization which runs through it'.

Trilling attributes this theme to Nietzsche and Freud but most of all to Frazer: 'I asked myself what books of the age just preceding ours had most influenced our literature … It was virtually inevitable that the first work that should have sprung to mind was Sir James Frazer's *The Golden Bough*. Anyone who thinks about modern literature in a systematic way takes for granted the great part played in it by myth, and especially by those examples of myth which tell us about gods dying and being reborn'. (This theme holds for both versions of Frazer's myth-ritualism.) Where Frazer is conventionally read as scorning myth and religion as outdated primitive counterparts to science, itself exclusively modern, Trilling reads him as *celebrating* the 'primitivism' that scientific modernity has lost: 'Scientific though his purpose was, Frazer had the effect of validating those old modes of experiencing the world which modern men, beginning with the Romantics, have sought to revive in order to escape from positivism and common sense'. For Trilling, Frazer espouses primitivism *against* civilization, and the heart of primitivism is myth.

For Trilling, modernists do not find the primitive *in* the modern. On the contrary, they reject the modern for the primitivism described by Frazer. In *The Literary Impact of 'The Golden Bough'* (1973) American literary critic John Vickery similarly traces the influence of Frazer's key themes on the chief modernists in English literature: Yeats, Eliot, Lawrence, and Joyce. The titles of his chapters make clear Vickery's focus on Frazer's theory of myth—for example, 'James Joyce: *Ulysses* and the Human Scapegoat'.

Frazer is hardly the only theorist of myth enlisted by modern writers. For example, in *Ancient Myth in Modern Poetry* (1971) American literary critic Lillian Feder shows the influence of Freud and Jung as well as of Frazer on, above all, Yeats, Pound, Eliot, and Auden. Of the influence of Freud and Jung, she writes: 'All these poets reflect the new awareness that myth is a guide to and expression of unconscious feelings and instincts'. She credits Frazer with 'discover[ing] behind ancient and primitive rites assumptions and patterns of thought and feeling that persist in some form throughout man's social history'.

For Feder, as for Vickery and as for Trilling, the influence of myth on literature is to be found not in allusions to ancient figures or events but in themes. Those themes are eternal. Myth remains germane to literature because myth, rightly grasped, is not about the fall of Troy or the fall of Jericho but about human nature.

Above all, for Feder, Vickery, and Trilling, the influence of myth on literature is the influence of *theories* of myth on literature. Myth is influential on writers because of what theorists find in myth.

The mythic origin of literature

Another form of the relationship between myth and literature already noted in Chapter 4 is the derivation of literature from myth—an approach pioneered by Jane Harrison and her fellow classicists Gilbert Murray and F. M. Cornford. Let's take some examples of this approach.

In *From Ritual to Romance* the English medievalist Jessie Weston (1850–1928) applied Frazer's second myth-ritualist version to the Grail legend. Following Frazer, she maintains that for ancients and primitives alike the fertility of the land depended on the fertility of their king, in whom resided the god of vegetation. But whereas for Frazer the key ritual was the replacement of an ailing king, for Weston the aim of the Grail quest was the *rejuvenation* of the ailing king. Furthermore, Weston adds an ethereal, spiritual dimension that transcends Frazer. The aim of the quest turns out to have been mystical oneness with god and not just food from god. It is this spiritual dimension of the legend that inspired T. S. Eliot to use Weston in 'The Waste Land'. Weston is not reducing the Grail legend to primitive myth and ritual but is merely tracing the legend back to primitive myth and ritual. The legend itself is literature, not myth. Because Frazer's second myth-ritualist scenario is not about the enactment of any myth of the god of vegetation but about the condition of the reigning king, the myth giving rise to the legend is not the life of a god like Adonis but the life of the Grail king himself.

In *The Idea of a Theater* Francis Fergusson (1904–86), an esteemed American theatre critic, applied Frazer's second myth-ritualist version to the whole genre of tragedy. He argues that the story of the suffering and redemption of the tragic hero derives from Frazer's scenario of the killing and replacement of the king. For example, Oedipus, King of Thebes, must sacrifice his throne, though not his life, for the sake of his subjects. Only with his abdication will the plague cease. But for Fergusson, as for Weston, the renewal sought is less physical than spiritual, and for Fergusson, Oedipus seeks it for himself as well as for his people.

More than most other literary myth-ritualists, Fergusson is concerned as much with the product—drama—as with the source—myth and ritual. He even criticizes Harrison and especially Murray for taking the meaning of tragedy to be the Frazerian act of regicide rather than, say, the theme of self-sacrifice. For Fergusson, as for Weston, the Frazerian scenario provides the background to literature but is itself myth and ritual rather than literature.

In *Anatomy of Criticism* famed Canadian literary critic Northrop Frye (1912–91) argued that not one genre but all genres of literature derive from myth—specifically, the myth of the life of the hero. Frye associates the life cycle of the hero with several other cycles: the yearly cycle of the seasons, the daily cycle of the sun, and the nightly cycle of dreaming and awakening. The association with the seasons comes from Frazer. The association with the sun, never attributed, perhaps comes from Max Müller. The association with dreaming comes from Jung. The association of the seasons with heroism, while again never attributed, may come from Raglan, who will shortly be considered in his own right. Frye offers his own heroic pattern, which he calls the 'quest-myth', but it consists of just four broad stages: the birth, triumph, isolation, and defeat of the hero.

For Frye, each main genre of literature parallels at once a season, a stage in the day, a stage of consciousness, and above all a stage in the heroic myth. Romance parallels at once spring, sunrise, awakening, and the birth of the hero. Comedy parallels summer, midday, waking consciousness, and the triumph of the hero. Tragedy parallels autumn, sunset, daydreaming, and the isolation of the hero. Satire parallels winter, night, sleep, and the defeat of the hero. The literary genres do not merely parallel the heroic myth but derive from it. The myth itself derives from ritual—from the second version of Frazer's myth-ritualism, the version in which divine kings are killed and replaced.

Like most other literary myth-ritualists, Frye does not reduce literature to myth. On the contrary, he, most uncompromisingly of all, insists on the autonomy of literature. Like Fergusson, he faults Murray and Cornford not for speculating about the myth-ritualist origin of tragedy (Murray) and comedy (Cornford)—a non-literary issue—but for interpreting the meaning of both as the enactment of Frazer's scenario of regicide—the literary issue.

Yet Frye proceeds to enlist both Frazer and Jung to help extricate the meaning, not just the origin, of literature. For he takes their key works to be themselves chiefly works of literary criticism rather than of anthropology or psychology:

> the fascination which *The Golden Bough* and Jung's book on libido symbols [i.e., *Symbols of Transformation* (Jung's Collected Works, vol. 5)] have for literary critics is…based…on the fact that these books are primarily studies in literary criticism.… *The Golden Bough* isn't really about what people did in a remote and savage past; it is about what human imagination does when it tries to express itself about the greatest mysteries, the mysteries of life and death and afterlife.

Similarly, Jung's *Psychology and Alchemy* (Jung's Collected Works, vol. 12), which Frye also singles out,

> is not a mere specious paralleling of a defunct science [i.e., alchemy] and one of several Viennese schools of psychology, but a grammar of literary symbolism which for all serious students of literature is as important as it is endlessly fascinating.

71

Because Frye brings myth and literature so closely together, even without collapsing literature into myth, his brand of literary criticism is confusingly called 'myth criticism', of which he himself is often considered the grandest practitioner. Equally commonly, his kind of literary criticism is called 'archetypal criticism' because in innocently calling the genres of literature 'archetypes', he is mistaken for a Jungian and, again, even the grandest of practitioners. To compound the confusion, there *are* outright Jungian literary critics who are aptly called archetypal critics, beginning with Maud Bodkin in *Archetypal Patterns in Poetry*. To compound the confusion yet further, there are post-Jungians who call themselves 'archetypal psychologists' *rather than* Jungians. The most prominent are James Hillman and David Miller, both of whom write voluminously on myth.

In *Violence and the Sacred* and other works René Girard, whose theory was discussed in Chapter 4, offers the sharpest break between myth and literature. Like Fergusson and Frye, Girard faults Harrison and Murray for conflating myth and ritual with tragedy. But he faults the two even more sternly for domesticating tragedy. For Harrison and Murray, myth merely *describes* the Frazerian ritual, and tragedy merely *dramatizes* it. Worse, tragedy turns an actual event into a mere theme. For Girard, myth covers up the ritual, and tragedy, as in Sophocles' plays about Oedipus, *uncovers* it. The function of myth is thus the opposite of the function of literature, or tragedy—a most original view of their relationship. Girard's criticism, however, is directed at Frazer's second myth-ritualist scenario, in which the king is outright killed. Harrison and Murray use instead Frazer's first myth-ritualist scenario, in which the king merely plays the part of the god of vegetation. In that scenario the god dies but the king does not, and the god may die without being killed, as in Adonis' annual trek to Hades. Girard's charge that Harrison, Murray, and even in part Frazer miss the human killing that underlies all tragedy does not in fact apply to them.

Myth as plot

Another aspect of myth as literature has been the focus on a common plot, or pattern. Nowhere in Tylor or Frazer is there any consideration of myth as other than plot. Terms that are formally distinguished from plot, if informally equated with it, are text, story, and narrative. Text means the 'script'. In the myth of Noah the text is Genesis 6–9.

Story means the events presented, but not necessarily in chronological order. There can be background events and digressions. In the case of Noah the story includes the emergence of the Nephilim and the general wickedness of almost all humanity, the corruption of the world itself, and the violation of the covenant between God and humanity. After the flood there is also Noah's getting drunk and being seen naked by one of his sons and the punishment of the descendants of that son.

Plot, often extracted from the story, is the causal chain of events. The plot of Noah is God's decision to destroy the world, to instruct Noah to build an ark to survive the flood, and then to repopulate the world.

Narrative is the choice of events told, in what order, and from what point of view. There can be an explicit narrator or an implicit one. In the case of Noah the implicit narrator is God, if only because the myth purportedly constitutes a verbatim revelation to Moses from God. By contrast, Homer and Hesiod are explicit narrators. From the Muses they seek the literary ability to tell their tales, but they are the tellers. Hesiod especially deems himself a poor farmer who has to cope with not only a harsh environment but also a wayward brother.

It is not that either Tylor or Frazer would deny that myth is more than plot. It is, rather, that both deem myth a causal explanation of events that merely happens to take the form of a plot. Their paralleling of myth to science requires the downplaying of the literary form and the playing up of the explanatory content. What interests Tylor and Frazer is the information itself, not the way it is conveyed. Standard literary considerations, such as characterization, time, voice, point of view, and reader response, are ignored, just as they would be in the analysis of a scientific law. (The contemporary focus in science on models and metaphors long postdates Tylor and Frazer.)

Because myth for Tylor and Frazer is intended to explain recurrent events, it can be rephrased as a law. For example: Whenever rain falls, it falls because the god of rain has decided to send it, and always for the same reason. When the sun rises, it rises because the sun god has chosen to mount his chariot, to which the sun is attached, and to drive the chariot across the sky, and again always for the same reason. Frazer sometimes takes the gods as symbols of natural processes, in which case myth rephrased is merely descriptive and not explanatory: myth is saying *that* rain falls (regularly or not) or *that* the sun rises (regularly) but not *why*.

Tylor, by contrast, always reads myth literally. He assumes that myth taken symbolically turns it into literature, which for him trivializes myth by turning an explanation of a natural process into a merely poetic description of that process. Where Frye and others argue that literature is not reducible to myth, Tylor argues that myth is not reducible to literature. In the wake of postmodernism, in which arguments in all fields, including science and law, are re-characterized as literature, Tylor's indifference to the literary aspects of myth is notable.

Tylor's separation of myth from literature is no less notable when seen from the standpoint of the American literary critic Kenneth Burke (1897–1993). In, above all, *The Rhetoric of Religion* Burke argues that myth is the transformation of metaphysics into literature. Myth expresses symbolically, in terms of temporal priority, what cannot be expressed literally: metaphysical priority. In Burke's famous phrase, myth is the 'temporizing of essence'. For example, the first creation myth in Genesis puts in the form of six days what in fact is the 'classification' of things in the world into six categories:

> Thus, instead of saying 'And that completes the first broad division, or classification, of our subject matter,' we'd say: 'And the evening and the morning were the first day.'

While myth for Burke is ultimately the expression of atemporal truths, it is still the expression of them in literary form, so that even if the meaning needs to be extricated from the form, story is still what makes myth myth. Here Burke is like Lévi-Strauss, whose approach to myth will be considered in Chapter 7. What Burke calls 'essence', Lévi-Strauss calls 'structure'.

Even more opposed to Tylor's downplaying of myth as story is the emphasis on myth as story by the 20th-century German philosopher Hans Blumenberg (1920–96). Where Tylor asserts that myth is an explanation that merely takes the form of a story, Blumenberg maintains that myth is a story and therefore not an explanation. Blumenberg asserts that myths tell stories *rather than* give reasons: 'In the [erroneous] etiological explanation of myth...the recognition of myth as an archaic accomplishment of reason has to be justified by its having initially and especially given answers to questions, rather than having [in actuality] been the implied rejection of those questions by means of storytelling'.

Blumenberg contends that within a myth anything can derive from anything else, in which case there must be scant interest in accurate derivation and therefore in explanation itself: 'When anything can be derived from anything, then there just is no explaining, and no demand for explanation. One just tells stories'. For Blumenberg, myth presents mere 'sequences rather than 'chronology', by which he means causality.

Against Blumenberg, one might argue, following Tylor, that story is simply the form that explanation takes. Plato, Plotinus, and other ancient critics of myth *as* story still take for granted that the function of myth in Homer and Hesiod is explanatory. Against Blumenberg, one might also argue that even if in myth anything can derive from anything else, so that nearly anything can happen, myth is still reporting how something did derive from something else and so how something did happen. Furthermore, Tylor maintains that there is more regularity in myth than is usually assumed. The clearest expression of regularity is patterns in the story.

Mythic patterns

Common plots, or patterns, have been proposed for, most often, hero myths. Other categories of myths, such as creation myths, flood myths, myths of paradise, and myths of the future, have proved too disparate for all but the broadest commonalities. Tylor specifies only that myths tell how a god decides to cause a natural event, but not what the god controls, what the god is like, or how the god acts. Narrowing his focus to gods of vegetation, Frazer specifies only that they die and are reborn, not how either occurs.

Yet our same Tylor, surprisingly turning briefly from myths about gods to hero myths, argued that repeatedly the hero is exposed at birth, is saved by other humans or animals, and grows up to become a national hero. Tylor seeks only to establish a common pattern. He does not apply to hero myths his theory of the origin, function, and subject matter of myths generally. Nevertheless, he appeals to the uniformity of the pattern to claim that whatever the origin, function, or subject matter of hero myths is, it must be the same in all hero myths to account for the similarity in plot:

> The treatment of similar myths from different regions, by arranging them in large compared groups, makes it possible to trace in

mythology the operation of imaginative processes recurring with the evident regularity of mental law.

Where Frye attributes myth to untethered imagination, Tylor attributes it to imagination subject to rigid cognitive constraints— the opposite of Blumemberg's assertion that anything can happen in myth. Tylor's claim is a prescient foreshadowing of present-day cognitive psychology.

In 1876 the Austrian scholar Johann Georg von Hahn used fourteen cases to argue that all 'Aryan' hero tales follow an 'exposure and return' formula more comprehensive than Tylor's. In each case the hero is born illegitimately, is abandoned by his father out of the fear of the prophecy of his future greatness, is saved by animals and raised by a lowly couple, fights wars, returns home triumphant, defeats his persecutors, frees his mother, becomes king, founds a city, and dies young. Though himself a solar mythologist, von Hahn, like Tylor, tried only to establish a pattern for hero myths. Had he proceeded to theorize about the tales, his theory would have rested on the commonality of the plot.

Similarly, in 1928 the Russian folklorist Vladimir Propp sought to demonstrate that Russian fairy tales follow a common plot, in which the hero goes off on a successful adventure and upon his return marries and gains the throne. Propp's pattern skirts both the birth and the death of the hero. While himself a Marxist, Propp here, in his earlier, formalist phase, attempted no more than Tylor and von Hahn: to establish a pattern for hero stories. But again, any theoretical salvo would have depended on the commonality of the plot.

Of the scholars who have theorized about the patterns that they have delineated in hero myths, the most important have been the Viennese psychoanalyst Otto Rank (1884–1939), the American mythographer Joseph Campbell (1904–87), and the English folklorist Lord Raglan (1885–1964). Rank later broke irreparably with Sigmund Freud, but when he wrote *The Myth of the Birth of the Hero* (1909), he was a Freudian apostle. While Campbell was never a full-fledged Jungian, he wrote *The Hero with a Thousand Faces* (1949) as a kindred soul of C. G. Jung. Raglan wrote *The Hero* (1936) as a Frazerian. Rank's and Campbell's works will be considered in detail in Chapter 6, on myth and psychology. Let us here take Raglan's as an illustration of the centrality of plot.

Lord Raglan

Raglan takes Frazer's second myth-ritualist version and applies it to myths about heroes. Where Frazer identifies the king with the god of vegetation, Raglan in turn identifies the king with the hero. For Frazer, the king's willingness to die for the community may be heroic, but Raglan outright labels it heroic. Frazer presents a simple pattern for the myth of the god: the god dies and is reborn. Raglan works out a detailed, twenty-two step pattern for the myth of the hero—a pattern he then applies to twenty-one myths (Box 1). But Raglan does more: he links up the myth with the ritual. Recall that in Frazer's second version the ritual enacted is not the myth of the death and rebirth of a god but the sheer transfer of the soul of the god from one king to another. There is really no myth at all. Raglan, by making the heart of hero myths not the attainment of the throne but the loss of it, matches the myth of the hero with the Frazerian ritual of the removal of the king. The king in the myth who loses his throne and later his life parallels the king in the ritual who loses both at once. The myth that Raglan links to ritual is not that of a god but that of a hero— some legendary figure whose selflessness real kings are expected to emulate. Strictly, then, the myth is less the *script* for the ritual, as in Frazer's first myth-ritualist scenario, than the *inspiration* for the ritual.

Box 1 Raglan's hero myth pattern, from *The Hero*

(1) The hero's mother is a royal virgin;

(2) His father is a king, and

(3) Often a near relative of his mother, but

(4) The circumstances of his conception are unusual, and

(5) He is also reputed to be the son of a god.

(6) At birth an attempt is made, usually by his father or his maternal grandfather, to kill him, but

(7) He is spirited away, and

(8) Reared by foster-parents in a far country.

(9) We are told nothing of his childhood, but

(10) On reaching manhood he returns or goes to his future kingdom.

(11) After a victory over the king and/or a giant, dragon, or wild beast,

(12) He marries a princess, often the daughter of his predecessor, and

(13) Becomes king.

(14) For a time he reigns uneventfully, and

(15) Prescribes laws, but

(16) Later he loses favour with the gods and/or his subjects, and

(17) Is driven from the throne and city, after which

(18) He meets with a mysterious death,

(19) Often at the top of a hill.

(20) His children, if any, do not succeed him.

(21) His body is not buried, but nevertheless

(22) He has one or more holy sepulchres.

Unlike the patterns of Tylor, Propp, or, as we shall see, either Rank or Campbell, Raglan's, like von Hahn's, covers the whole of the hero's life.

Raglan equates the hero of the myth with the god of the ritual. First, the king connects the hero to the god: heroes are kings, and kings are gods. Second, many of the events in the life of the hero are superhuman, especially points 5 and 11. True, the hero must die, but his death accomplishes a god-like feat: reviving vegetation. Third, in both the myth and the ritual the removal of the king ensures the survival of the community, which would otherwise starve. In both myth and ritual the king is a saviour.

Doubtless Raglan would never expect Adonis to fit his pattern, even though Adonis is one of Frazer's main examples in his first version of myth-ritualism. While points 1 through 4 seem to fit snugly, few of the others fit at all. For example, there is an attempt on the life of Adonis' mother but no attempt on Adonis' own life, at least at the outset (point 6). Perhaps Adonis can be said to have been raised by foster parents—Aphrodite and Persephone—and in a distant land (point 8), but not because he has been spirited away

7. The Duke and Duchess of Windsor on their wedding day, June 1937, after Edward's abdication.

(point 7). Most important, Adonis never becomes king and so has no throne to lose. He does lose his life, but not while reigning as king, or even while living in a society. Of all of Raglan's chosen examples, the one that fits best is Oedipus. A biblical hero who would fit almost as well is King Saul. Unlike Frazer, Raglan is too timid to mention the case of Jesus. A modern example would be King Edward VIII of England, the heart of whose life was his abdication (see Figure 7).

What matters in this chapter is the centrality of the plot to Raglan's theory. Raglan appeals to the commonality of the plot to argue that the meaning of hero myths lies in that common plot, that the heart of the common plot is the loss of the throne, and that only an accompanying ritual of regicide makes sense of the common focus in the myth on the toppling of the king. Raglan's myth-ritualism does not merely make the plot the scenario for the ritual but argues for the ritual from the plot.

Chapter 6
Myth and psychology

There are multiple theories in each discipline that have contributed to the study of myth. In psychology, two theories have almost, though not quite, monopolized the field: those of the Viennese physician Sigmund Freud (1856–1939) and of the Swiss psychiatrist C. G. Jung (1875–1961).

Sigmund Freud

While Freud analyses myths throughout his writings, his main discussion of his key myth, that of Oedipus, fittingly occurs in *The Interpretation of Dreams*, for he, and Jung as well, parallel myths to dreams:

> If *Oedipus Rex* moves a modern audience no less than it did the contemporary Greek one, the explanation can only be that its effect does not lie in the contrast between destiny and human [free] will, but is to be looked for in the particular nature of the material on which that contrast is exemplified. There must be something [latent] which makes a voice within us ready to recognize the compelling force of destiny in the *Oedipus*. . . . His [Oedipus'] destiny moves us only because it might have been ours—because the oracle laid the same curse upon us before our birth as upon him. . . . Our dreams convince us that that is so. King

Oedipus, who slew his father Laïus and married his mother Jocasta, merely shows us the fulfilment of our own childhood wishes. But, more fortunate than he, we have meanwhile succeeded, in so far as we have not become psychoneurotics, in detaching our sexual impulses from our mothers and in forgetting our jealousy of our fathers.

On the surface, or manifest, level, the story of Oedipus describes that figure's vain effort to elude the fate that has been imposed on him. Latently, however, Oedipus most wants to do what manifestly he least wants to do. He wants to act out his 'Oedipus complex'. The manifest, or literal, level of the myth hides the latent, symbolic meaning. On the manifest level Oedipus is the innocent victim of Fate. On the latent level he is the culprit. Rightly understood, the myth depicts not Oedipus' failure to circumvent his ineluctable destiny but his success in fulfilling his fondest desires.

Yet the latent meaning scarcely stops here. For the myth is not ultimately about Oedipus at all. Just as the manifest level, on which Oedipus is the victim, masks a latent one, on which Oedipus is the victimizer, so that level in turn masks an even more latent one, on which the real victimizer is the myth-maker and any reader of the myth grabbed by it. Here the myth is about the fulfilment of the Oedipus complex in the male myth-maker or reader, who identifies himself with Oedipus and through him fulfils his own Oedipus complex. At heart, the myth is not biography but autobiography.

In whom does the Oedipus complex lie? To a degree it lies in all adult males, none of whom has fully outgrown the desires that first arose in childhood. But the complex lies above all in neurotic adult males who are stuck, or fixated, at their Oedipal stage. For many reasons they cannot fulfil their desires directly. Their parents may no longer be alive or, if alive, may no longer be so intimidating or so alluring. Furthermore, surely not even the most indulgent parents would readily consent. Any son who did succeed would likely get caught and punished. And the guilt felt for having killed the father whom one loved as much as hated, and for having forced oneself upon a resisting mother, would be overwhelming. But the biggest obstacle to the enactment of the complex is more fundamental. One does not know that the complex exists. It has been repressed.

Under these circumstances, myth provides the ideal kind of fulfilment. True, the outer layers of the myth hide its true meaning and thereby block fulfilment, but they simultaneously reveal that true meaning and thereby provide fulfilment. After all, on even the literal level Oedipus does kill his father and does have sex with his mother. He simply does so unintentionally. If on the next level it is Oedipus rather than the myth-maker or reader who acts intentionally, the action is still intentional. The level above therefore partly reveals, even as it partly hides, the meaning below. The true meaning always lies at the level below but is always conveyed by the level above. By identifying themselves with Oedipus, neurotic adult males secure a partial fulfilment of their own lingering Oedipal desires, but without becoming conscious of those desires. Myth thus constitutes a compromise between the side of oneself that wants the desires satisfied outright and the side that does not even want to know they exist. For Freud, myth functions *through* its meaning: myth vents Oedipal desires by presenting a story in which, symbolically, they are enacted.

In all these ways myths parallel dreams, which, like science for Tylor and Frazer, provide the model by which Freud and Jung analyse myths. To be sure, there are differences between myths and dreams. Where dreams are private, myths are public. Where for Freud myths are limited to neurotics, dreams are universal. But for Freud and Jung alike the similarities are more significant.

Otto Rank

The classic Freudian analyses of myth are Karl Abraham's *Dreams and Myths* and Otto Rank's *The Myth of the Birth of the Hero*. Both Abraham and Rank follow the master in comparing myths with dreams—the title of Abraham's book says it all—and in deeming both the disguised, symbolic fulfilment of repressed, overwhelmingly Oedipal wishes lingering in the adult myth-maker or reader. But Rank considers more myths, analyses them in more detail, and most of all presents a common plot, or pattern, for one category of myths: those of heroes, specifically male heroes. Freudians analyse all kinds of myths, not just hero myths. Even creation myths have been seen as accomplishing the feat of giving birth to the world—by males as well as by females.

For Rank, following Freud, heroism deals with what *Jungians* call the 'first half of life'. The first half—birth, childhood, adolescence, and young adulthood—involves the establishment of oneself as an independent person in the external world. The attainment of independence expresses itself concretely in the securing of a job and a mate. The securing of either requires both separation from one's parents and mastery of one's instincts. Independence of parents means not the rejection of them but self-sufficiency. Similarly, independence of instincts means not the denial of them but control over them. When Freud says that the test of happiness is the capacity to work and love, he is clearly referring to the goals of the first half of life, which for him hold for all of life. Freudian problems involve a lingering attachment to either parents or instincts. To depend on one's parents for the satisfaction of instincts, or to satisfy instincts in antisocial ways, is to be fixated at a childish level of psychological development.

Rank's pattern (Box 2), which he applies to over thirty hero myths, falls within the first half of life. Roughly paralleling Johann Georg von Hahn's pattern, which was mentioned in Chapter 5 and of

Box 2 Rank's hero myth pattern, from *The Myth of the Birth of the Hero*

The standard saga itself may be formulated according to the following outline: The hero is the child of most distinguished parents, usually the son of a king. His origin is preceded by difficulties, such as continence, or prolonged barrenness, or secret intercourse of the parents due to external prohibition or obstacles. During or before the pregnancy, there is a prophecy, in the form of a dream or oracle, cautioning against his birth, and usually threatening danger to the father (or his representative). As a rule, he is surrendered to the water, in a box. He is then saved by animals, or by lowly people (shepherds), and is suckled by a female animal or by an humble woman. After he has grown up, he finds his distinguished parents, in a highly versatile fashion. He takes his revenge on his father, on the one hand, and is acknowledged, on the other. Finally he achieves rank and honors.

which he was apparently unaware, Rank's goes from the hero's birth to his attainment of a 'career'.

Literally, or consciously, the hero is a historical or legendary figure like Oedipus. He is heroic because he rises from obscurity to, typically, the throne. Literally, he is an innocent victim of either his parents or Fate. While his parents have yearned for a child and decide to sacrifice him only to save the father, they nevertheless do decide to sacrifice him. The hero's revenge, if the parricide is even committed knowingly, is, then, understandable: who would not consider killing one's would-be killer?

Symbolically, or unconsciously, the hero is heroic not because he dares to win a throne but because he dares to kill his father. The killing is definitely intentional, and the cause is not revenge but sexual frustration. The father has refused to surrender his wife—the real object of the son's efforts:

as a rule the deepest, generally unconscious root of the dislike of the son for the father, or of two brothers for each other, is referable to the competition for the tender devotion and love of the mother.

Too horrendous to face, the true meaning of the hero myth is covered up by the concocted story, which makes the father, not the son, the culprit. The pattern is simply

the excuse, as it were, for the hostile feelings which the child harbors against his father, and which in this fiction are projected against the father.

What the hero seeks gets masked as power, not incest. Most of all, who the hero is becomes some third party—the named hero—rather than either the creator of the myth or anyone stirred by it. Identifying himself with the named hero, the myth-maker or reader vicariously revels in the hero's triumph, which in fact is his own. *He* is the real hero of the myth.

Literally, the myth culminates in the hero's attainment of a throne. Symbolically, the hero gains a mate as well. One might, then, conclude that the myth aptly expresses the Freudian goal of the first half of life. In actuality, it expresses the opposite. The wish fulfilled is not for detachment from one's parents and from one's anti-social instincts but, on the contrary, for the most intense possible relationship to one's parents and for the most antisocial of urges: parricide and incest, even rape. Taking one's father's job and one's mother's hand does not quite spell independence of them.

The myth-maker or reader is an adult, but the wish vented by the myth is that of a child of three to five. The fantasy is the fulfilment of the Oedipal wish to kill one's father in order to gain access to one's mother. The myth fulfils a wish never outgrown by the adult who either invents or uses the myth. That adult is psychologically an eternal child. Having never developed an ego strong enough to master his instincts, he is neurotic. Since no mere child can overpower his father, the myth-maker imagines being old enough to do so. In short, the myth expresses not the Freudian goal of the first half of life but the fixated childhood goal that keeps one from accomplishing it.

To be sure, the fulfilment of the Oedipal wish is symbolic rather than literal, disguised rather than overt, unconscious rather than conscious, mental rather than physical, and vicarious rather than direct. By identifying himself with the named hero, the creator or reader of the myth acts out in his mind deeds that he would never dare act out in the world. Even the Oedipal deeds of the *named* hero are disguised, for the heroic pattern operates at or near the manifest, not the latent, level. Still, the myth does provide fulfilment of a kind and, in light of the conflict between the neurotic's impulses and the neurotic's morals, provides the best possible fulfilment. Rank contrasts the neurotic, who has repressed his impulses and so needs an indirect outlet for them, to the 'pervert', who acts out his impulses and so presumably has no need of any halfway measure like myth.

Jacob Arlow

Mainstream psychoanalysis has changed considerably since Rank's *Myth of the Birth of the Hero*. Led by the development of ego psychology, which has expanded the scope of psychoanalysis from abnormal to normal personality, contemporary psychoanalysts like the American Jacob Arlow (1912–2004) see myth as contributing to normal development rather than to the perpetuation of neurosis. For them, myth helps one to grow up rather than, like Peter Pan, to remain a child. Myth abets adjustment to the social and the physical worlds rather than childish flight from them. Myth may still serve to fulfil wishes of the id, or the part of the mind from which instinctual impulses arise, but it serves far more the functions of the ego—defence and adaptation—and of the superego—renunciation. Furthermore, myth for contemporary psychoanalysts serves everyone, not merely neurotics. Put summarily, contemporary psychoanalysts take myth positively rather than, like classical ones, negatively. To quote Arlow:

> Psychoanalysis has a greater contribution to make to the study of mythology than [merely] demonstrating, in myths, wishes often encountered in the unconscious thinking of patients. The myth is a particular kind of communal experience. It is a special form of shared fantasy, and it serves to bring the individual into relationship with members of his cultural group on the basis of certain common needs. Accordingly, the myth can be studied from the point of view of its function in psychic integration—how it plays a role in warding off feelings of guilt and anxiety, how it constitutes a form of adaptation to reality and to the group in which the individual lives, and how it influences the crystallization of the individual identity and the formation of the superego.

Where for classical Freudians myths are like dreams, for contemporary psychoanalysts myths are unlike them. Dreams still serve to satisfy wishes, but myths serve either to deny or to sublimate them. For classical Freudians, myths are simply public dreams. For contemporary psychoanalysts, myths, *because* public, serve to socialize.

Bruno Bettelheim

In his bestselling book *The Uses of Enchantment* the well-known contemporary psychoanalyst Bruno Bettelheim (1903–90), Viennese-born and eventually American-resident, says much the same as Arlow but says it of fairy tales *rather than* of myths, which he quirkily pits against fairy tales and interprets in a classical Freudian way. Classical Freudians tend to see myths and fairy tales as akin, just as they do myths and dreams. It is contemporary psychoanalysts who contrast myths to fairy tales, but usually they favour myths over fairy tales, seeing myths as serving the ego or the superego and seeing fairy tales as serving the id. (The key exception among classical Freudians to the paralleling of myths to fairy tales was the Hungarian anthropologist Géza Róheim [1891–1953], who contrasts myths to fairy tales, or folk tales, in a fashion that presciently anticipates Arlow.)

Bettelheim does the reverse of Arlow. To be sure, he does not consider myths to be wish fulfilments. Echoing Arlow, he maintains that

> Myths typically involve superego demands in conflict with id-motivated action, and with the self-preserving desires of the ego.

But for Bettelheim, in contrast to Arlow, the mythic superego is so unbending that the maturation it espouses is unattainable. Fairy tales no less than myths preach maturation, but they do so more gently and thereby succeed where myths fail. In myths the heroes, who are often gods, succeed only because they are exceptional. In fairy tales the heroes are ordinary persons, whose success inspires emulation. In short, myths for Bettelheim wind up hindering psychological growth, whereas fairy tales foster it.

Alan Dundes

Not all present-day Freudians have spurned the classical approach to myth. The pre-eminent American folklorist Alan Dundes (1935–2005) is defiantly old fashioned. For him, myth fulfils rather than renounces or sublimates repressed wishes. Declares Dundes:

> The content of folklore ... is largely unconscious. Hence it represents id, not ego, for the most part. From this perspective, ego psychology cannot possibly illuminate much of the content of folklore.

Dundes delights in demonstrating the hidden, antisocial wishes vented by myths—wishes that are as often anal as Oedipal, as often homosexual as heterosexual, and at times completely nonsexual.

C. G. Jung

Where for Freud and Rank heroism is limited to the first half of life, for C. G. Jung it involves the second half even more. For Freud and Rank, heroism involves relations with parents and instincts. For Jung, heroism involves, in addition, relations with the unconscious. In the first half of life heroism means separation not only from parents and antisocial instincts but even more from the unconscious: every child's managing to forge consciousness is for Jung a supremely heroic feat. Like Freudians, Jungians at once analyse all kinds of myths, not just hero myths, and interpret other kinds heroically. Creation myths, for example, symbolize the creation of consciousness out of the unconscious.

For Freud, the unconscious is the product of the repression of instincts. For Jung, it is inherited rather than created and includes far more than repressed instincts. Independence of the Jungian unconscious therefore means more than independence of instincts. It means the formation of consciousness, the object of which in the first half of life is the external world.

The goal of the uniquely Jungian second half of life is likewise consciousness, but now consciousness of the Jungian unconscious rather than of the external world. One must return to the unconscious, from which one has invariably become severed. But the aim is not thereby to sever one's ties to the external world. On the contrary, the aim is still to return to the external world. The ideal is a balance between consciousness of the external world and consciousness of the unconscious. The aim of the second half of life is to supplement, not abandon, the achievements of the first half.

Just as conventionally Freudian problems involve the failure to establish oneself externally, so distinctively Jungian problems involve the failure to re-establish oneself internally. Freudian problems stem from excessive attachment to the world of childhood. Jungian problems stem from excessive attachment to the world one enters upon breaking free of the childhood world: the external world. To be disconnected from the internal world is to feel empty and lost.

Joseph Campbell

Jung himself allows for heroism in both halves of life, but Joseph Campbell, whose *Hero with a Thousand Faces* provides the classical Jungian counterpart to Rank's *Myth of the Birth of the Hero*, does not. Just as Rank confines heroism to the first half of life, so Campbell restricts it to the second half (Box 3).

Rank's scheme begins with the hero's birth; Campbell's, with his adventure. Where Rank's scheme ends, Campbell's begins: with the adult hero ensconced at home. Rank's hero must be young enough for his father still to be reigning. Campbell does not specify the age of his hero, but the hero must be no younger than the age at which

> ### Box 3 Campbell's hero myth pattern, from *The Hero with a Thousand Faces*
>
> *The standard path of the mythological adventure of the hero is a magnification of the formula represented in the rites of passage: separation–initiation–return: which might be named the nuclear unit of the monomyth.*
>
> *A hero ventures forth from the world of common day into a region of supernatural wonder: fabulous forces are there encountered and a decisive victory is won: the hero comes back from this mysterious adventure with the power to bestow boons on his fellow man.*

Rank's hero myth ends: young adulthood. He must, again, be in the second half of life. Campbell does acknowledge heroism in the first half of life and even cites Rank's *Myth of the Birth of the Hero*, but he demotes this youthful heroism to mere preparation for adult heroism. Antithetically to Jung, he dismisses birth itself as unheroic because it is not done consciously!

Rank's hero must be the son of royal or at least distinguished parents. Campbell's can be of any class. Campbell cites at least as many female heroes as male ones, even though stage two of his pattern—initiation—necessitates male heroes! Likewise some of his heroes are young, even though his pattern requires adult heroes! Finally, Campbell's pattern commits him to human heroes, even though some of his heroes are divine! Rank's pattern, by contrast, allows for divine as well as human heroes.

Where Rank's hero returns to his birthplace, Campbell's marches forth to a strange, divine world which the hero has never even known existed:

> This fateful region of both treasure and danger may be variously represented: as a distant land, a forest, a kingdom underground, beneath the waves, or above the sky, a secret island, lofty mountaintop, or profound dream state.

This extraordinary world is the world of the gods, and the hero must hail from the human world precisely for the worlds to stand in contrast.

In this exotic, supernatural world the hero encounters above all a supreme female god and a supreme male god. The maternal goddess is loving and caring:

> She is the paragon of all paragons of beauty, the reply to all desire, the bliss-bestowing goal of every hero's earthly and unearthly quest.

By contrast, the male god is tyrannical and merciless—an 'ogre'. The hero, who here must be male, has sex with the goddess and marries her. He fights the god, either before or after his encounter with the goddess. Yet with both, not just the goddess, he becomes mystically one and thereby becomes divine himself.

Where Rank's hero *returns* home to encounter his father and mother, Campbell's hero *leaves* home to encounter a male and a female god, who are father- and mother-like but are not his parents. Yet the two heroes' encounters are remarkably akin: just as Rank's hero kills his father and, if usually below the level of the pattern, marries his mother, so Campbell's hero, even if often in reverse order, marries the goddess and fights, even if not kills, the god.

The differences, however, are even more significant. Because the goddess is not the hero's mother, sex with her does not constitute incest. Moreover, the two not only marry but also become mystically one. And despite appearances, the hero's relationship to the male god is for Campbell no less positive. The hero is really seeking from the father god the same love that he has just won or will soon win from the goddess. He seeks reconciliation, or 'atonement'.

When Campbell writes that the myths accompanying initiation rituals 'reveal the benign self-giving aspect of the *archetypal* father', he is using the term in its Jungian sense. For Freudians, gods symbolize parents. For Jungians, parents symbolize gods, who in turn symbolize father and mother archetypes, which are components of the hero's personality. The hero's relationship to these gods symbolizes not, as for Freud and Rank, a son's relationship to other persons—his parents—but the relationship of one side of a male's personality—his ego—to another side—his unconscious. The father and the mother are but two of the archetypes of which the Jungian, or 'collective', unconscious is composed. Archetypes are unconscious not because they have been repressed but because they have never become conscious. For Jung and Campbell, myth originates and functions not, as for Freud and Rank, to satisfy neurotic urges that cannot be manifested openly but to express normal sides of the personality that have just not had a chance at realization.

By identifying himself with the hero of a myth, Rank's male myth-maker or reader vicariously lives out in his mind an adventure that, if ever directly fulfilled, would be acted out on his parents themselves. By contrast, Campbell's male or female myth-maker or reader vicariously lives out mentally an adventure that even when directly fulfilled would still be taking place in the mind. For parts of the mind are what the hero is really encountering. In drug lingo, Campbell's heroic adventure amounts to 'tripping'.

Having managed to break free of the secure, everyday world and go off to a dangerous, divine one, Campbell's hero, to complete the journey, must in turn break free of the divine world, in which the hero has by now become ensconced, and return to the everyday one. So enticing is the divine world that leaving it proves harder than leaving home was. Circe, Calypso, the Sirens, and the Lotus Eaters thus tempt Odysseus with a carefree, immortal life.

Though often misconstrued, Jung no less than Freud opposes a state of sheer unconsciousness. Both strive to make the unconscious conscious. Jung opposes the rejection of ordinary, or ego, consciousness for unconsciousness as vigorously as he opposes the rejection of unconsciousness for ego consciousness. He seeks a balance between ego consciousness and the unconscious, between consciousness of the external world and consciousness of the unconscious. For Jung, the hero's failure to return to the everyday world would spell his failure to resist the allure of the unconscious.

By contrast, Campbell seeks pure unconsciousness. His hero never returns to the everyday world. He surrenders to the unconscious. Even though Campbell himself demands the hero's return to the everyday world, the world to which the hero returns *is* the divine world. No separate everyday world exists. The everyday world and the divine world are really one:

> The two worlds, the divine and the human [i.e., everyday], can be pictured only as distinct from each other—different as life and death, as day and night.... Nevertheless ... the two kingdoms are actually one.

Like Dorothy in 'The Wizard of Oz', the hero need never have left home after all. Where Jung espouses balance between ego consciousness and the unconscious, Campbell espouses fusion. Psychologically and metaphysically alike, hero myths for him preach mystical oneness.

Adonis

While Jung himself mentions Adonis only in passing, he does mention him as an instance of the archetype of the eternal child, or *puer aeternus*. From a Jungian point of view, the myth of Adonis serves as a warning to those who identify themselves with the archetype. To live as a *puer*, the way Adonis does, is to live as a psychological infant and, ultimately, as a foetus. The life of a *puer* in myth invariably ends in premature death, which psychologically means the death of the ego and a return to the womb-like unconscious.

As an archetype, the *puer* constitutes a side of one's personality, which, as a side, must be accepted. A *puer* personality simply goes too far: he makes the *puer* the whole of his personality. Unable to resist its spell, he surrenders himself to it, thereby abandoning his ego and reverting to sheer unconsciousness.

The reason a *puer* personality cannot resist the *puer* archetype is that he remains under the spell of the archetype of the Great Mother, who initially is identical with the unconscious as a whole. Unable to free himself from her, he never forges a strong, independent ego, without which he cannot in turn resist any smothering female he meets. His surrender to the *puer* archetype means his surrender to the Great Mother, to whom he yearns to return.

Biologically, a *puer* can range in age from adolescence, the period of the most dramatic expression, to middle or even old age. Psychologically, however, a *puer* is an infant. Where for Freud a person in the grip of an Oedipus complex is psychologically fixated at three to five years of age, for Jung a *puer* is fixated at birth. Where an Oedipus complex presupposes an independent ego 'egotistically' seeking to possess the mother for itself, a *puer* involves a tenuous ego seeking to surrender itself to the mother. A *puer* seeks not domination but absorption—and thereby reversion to the state prior even to birth.

For Freud, attachment to the mother at any stage means attachment to one's actual mother or mother substitute. For Jung, attachment to the mother means attachment to the mother archetype, of which one's actual mother or mother substitute is only a manifestation. Where for Freud a boy should free himself of his yearning, infantile or Oedipal, for his own mother, for Jung a boy should free himself of his inclination to identify himself with the mother archetype. For Freud, the failure to free oneself means eternal attachment to one's own mother. For Jung, it means the restriction of one's personality to the mother archetype within. Where for Freud the struggle for freedom is between one person and another—son and mother—for Jung it is between one part of a person and another—ego and unconscious, which, again, the mother archetype first symbolizes.

Because an archetype expresses itself only through symbols, never directly, the aspects of the mother archetype which a boy knows are only those filtered through his actual mother or mother substitute. A mother who refuses to let her son go limits him to only the smothering, negative side of the mother archetype. The mother archetype, as an archetype, is inherited. Experience determines only which aspects of the archetype are elicited. A boy who never experiences a positive, nourishing mother figure will never develop that dimension of the archetype latent in him.

Adonis is a quintessential *puer* because he never marries, never works, and dies young. He simply never grows up. He must first break out of a tree in order to be born. In Ovid's version his mother, transformed into the tree, is reluctant to let him out. Like any other mother, she may be overjoyed at his conception. But unlike normal mothers, she wants to hoard him. Adonis himself has to find an exit.

No sooner does Adonis emerge from the tree than, in Apollodorus' version, Aphrodite thrusts him back—not, to be sure, into the tree but into a chest. She thereby undoes the birth that had proved so arduous. When Persephone, to whom Aphrodite has entrusted the chest without revealing its contents, opens it, she likewise falls in love with Adonis and refuses to return him. Each goddess, just like his mother, wants to possess him exclusively. Though Zeus' decision leaves Adonis free for a third of the year, Adonis readily cedes his third to Aphrodite. Never, then, is he outside the custody of these archetypal mother figures.

Adonis is unable to resist the goddesses, but not because they arouse him sexually. He sees them not as irresistibly beautiful females but as his mother, with whom he seeks not sex but absorption. Between him and the goddesses there exists the primordial state of mystical oneness that Lucien Lévy-Bruhl, whom Jung often cites, calls *participation mystique* (see Chapter 1). Psychologically, Adonis is at exactly that stage of humanity which Lévy-Bruhl and, following him, Jung consider primitive. Where Campbell would laud Adonis' identification with the world as mystical, Jung condemns it as infantile.

Chapter 7
Myth and structure

Claude Lévi-Strauss

Claude Lévi-Strauss' contribution to the study of myth, first
considered in Chapter 1, was not only the revival of a Tylorian
view of myth as proto-scientific but, even more, the invention of a
'structuralist' approach to myth. Recall that for Lévi-Strauss myth
is an instance of thinking per se, modern or primitive, because it
classifies phenomena. Humans, argues Lévi-Strauss, think in the
form of classifications, specifically pairs of oppositions, and
project them onto the world. Not only myth and science, which
Lévi-Strauss treats as taxonomies, but also cooking, music, art,
literature, dress, etiquette, marriage, and economics evince
humanity's pairing impulse.

For Lévi-Strauss, the distinctiveness of myth among these
phenomena is threefold. First, myth is seemingly the least orderly
of them: 'It would seem that in the course of a myth anything is
likely to happen. There is [seemingly] no logic, no continuity'. To
be able to organize even myths into sets of oppositions would be to
prove irrefutably that order is inherent in all cultural phenomena
and that the mind must therefore underlie it. As Lévi-Strauss
declares at the outset of *Introduction to a Science of Mythology*,
his four-volume tome on Native American mythology:

The experiment I am now embarking on with mythology will consequently be more decisive.... [I]f it were possible to prove in this instance, too, that the apparent arbitrariness of the mind, its supposedly spontaneous flow of inspiration, and its seemingly uncontrolled inventiveness imply the existence of laws operating at a deeper level, we would inevitably be forced to conclude that when the mind is left to commune with itself and no longer has to come to terms with objects, it is in a sense reduced to imitating itself as object... [I]f the human mind appears determined even in the realm of mythology, *a fortiori* it must also be determined in all its spheres of activity.

Like Tylor, Lévi-Strauss appeals to the orderliness of the mind to prove that it stems from the scientific-like processes of observation and hypothesis rather than from unbounded imagination.

Second, myth, together with totemism, is the only exclusively primitive phenomenon among the ones that Lévi-Strauss considers. To prove that it is orderly would prove that its creator is orderly, hence logical and intellectual, as well.

Third and most important, myth alone not only expresses oppositions, which are equivalent to contradictions, but also resolves them: 'the purpose of myth is to provide a logical model capable of overcoming a contradiction'. Myth resolves or, more precisely, tempers a contradiction 'dialectically', by providing either a mediating middle term or an analogous, but more easily resolved, contradiction.

Like the contradictions expressed in other phenomena, those expressed in myth are of innumerable kinds. All, however, are apparently reducible to instances of the fundamental contradiction between 'nature' and 'culture', between humans as animals, and so a part of nature, and humans as distinctively human beings, and so a part of culture. That conflict is the projection onto the world of the oppositional character of the human mind. Humans not only think 'oppositionally' but consequently experience the world 'oppositionally' as well. It might, then, seem as if Lévi-Strauss, like Freud and Jung, makes the subject matter of myth the mind rather than the world. But in fact he does not. He is not, like them, seeking to identify projections in order to withdraw them. He is seeking simply to trace the source of them. In fact, Lévi-Strauss maintains that the world is itself organized 'oppositionally', so that human projections, while remaining projections, match the nature of the world. Jung maintains the same in his doctrine of synchronicity. Once Lévi-Strauss does trace the source of projections, he proceeds to deal with them as experiences of the world, so that the subject matter of myth for him, as for Bultmann, Jonas, and Camus, is the encounter with the world—but with the world experienced as contradictory rather than as akin or indifferent.

The clearest examples of the conflict between nature and culture are the recurrent oppositions that Lévi-Strauss finds between raw and cooked food, wild and tame animals, and incest and exogamy. It is much less clear how other oppositions that he finds—such as those between sun and moon, earth and sky, hot and cold, high and low, left and right, male and female, and life and death— symbolize the split between nature and culture rather than a split within nature. Similarly, it is far from clear how oppositions like those of sister versus wife and of matrilocal versus patrilocal kinship symbolize anything other than a split within culture.

Lévi-Strauss writes mainly about Native American myths, but best known is his analysis of the Oedipus myth, the first of the two myths he analyses in his programmatic 'Structural Study of Myth'. We are told that the Oedipus myth tempers an instance of the clash between nature and culture by noting that humans are able to tolerate a parallel case of the clash:

> Although the problem [i.e., the opposition] obviously cannot be solved [i.e., resolved], the Oedipus myth provides a kind of logical

tool which, to phrase it coarsely, replaces the original problem....By
a correlation of this type [i.e., of the original opposition with an
analogous one], the overrating of blood relations is to the
underrating of blood relations [i.e., the more easily tolerated
opposition] as the attempt to escape autochthony is to the
impossibility to succeed in it [i.e., the opposition needing
resolution].

Arranging the elements of the myth not in the chronological
order of the plot but in the recurrent order of two sets of
opposing pairs, Lévi-Strauss argues that the myth is ameliorating
the tension within one pair by juxtaposing it with a comparable
pair that is already accepted. The already accepted opposition
is that between the 'overrating' and the 'underrating' of 'blood
relations'. Overrating refers to either the commission of
incest (Oedipus' marrying his mother) or the violation of a
prohibition in the name of family (Antigone's burying her
brother Polynices). 'Underrating' refers to either fratricide
(Eteocles' killing his brother Polynices) or patricide (Oedipus'
killing his father). Overrating represents nature, for it is
instinctual. Underrating represents culture, for it is unnatural.
In taking on the myth of Oedipus, and in focusing on familial
sex and killing, Lévi-Strauss might appear to be following
Freud, but in fact he dismisses Freud's analysis as just one
more version of the myth itself rather than as even an inferior
analysis of it.

In the myth of Oedipus the opposition requiring acceptance is that
between the 'denial' and the 'affirmation' of 'autochthonous origin'.
Denial refers to the killing of earthborn monsters which either
prevent the birth of humans (Kadmos' killing the dragon, from the
extracted teeth of which humans are born) or threaten the survival
of humans (Oedipus' killing the Sphinx, which is starving Thebes).
Affirmation refers to the common mythological association of
humans born from the earth with difficulty in walking (Oedipus'
name meaning 'swollen footed'). To kill earthborn monsters is to

deny the connection of humans to the earth; to name humans on the basis of difficulty in walking is to affirm the connection of humans to the earth. Denial represents nature, for humans are in fact born from human parents rather than from the earth. Affirmation represents culture, for mythology maintains that humans are born from the earth. How ancient Greeks were able to tolerate the one set of oppositions more easily than the other, Lévi-Strauss never discloses.

Yet other myths fail to overcome oppositions to even this extent. They show instead that any alternative arrangement would be worse. The Tsimshian Native American myth of Asdiwal, for example, serves

> to justify the shortcomings [i.e., the contradictions] of reality, since the extreme [i.e., alternative] positions are only imagined in order to show that they are untenable.

Rather than resolving the contradiction between death and life, a myth makes death superior to immortality, or eternal life:

> The Indians of North America explain this by saying that if death did not exist, the earth would become overpopulated and there would not be room for everyone.

Because myth concerns the human experience of the world, not to say the deepest anxieties experienced in the world, it would seemingly have existential import, as myth does for Bultmann, Jonas, and Camus. Yet Lévi-Strauss, like Tylor, treats myth as a coldly intellectual phenomenon: the oppositions expressed in myth constitute logical puzzles rather than existential predicaments. Myth involves thinking, not feeling. At the same time myth involves more the process than the content of thinking. Here Lévi-Strauss anticipates the focus of contemporary cognitive psychologists.

In calling his approach to myth 'structuralist', Lévi-Strauss intends to distinguish it from the approach that adheres to the plot of myth. All other theories do so. To be sure, not all these theorists are equally interested in the plot. Lévy-Bruhl, for example, is concerned with the world view underlying it, but he still attributes a plot to myth. For Tylor, by contrast, the plot is central: myth presents the process by which events happen in the world.

Lévi-Strauss alone dispenses with the plot, or 'diachronic dimension', of myth and locates the meaning of myth in the structure, or 'synchronic dimension'. Where the plot of a myth is that event A leads to event B, which leads to event C, which leads to event D, the structure, which is identical with the expression and resolution of contradictions, is either that events A and B constitute an opposition mediated by event C or that events A and B, which constitute the same opposition, are to each other as events C and D, an analogous opposition, are to each other.

Every myth contains a series of oppositional sets, each composed of a pair of oppositions resolved one way or the other. The relationship among the sets matches that among the elements within each set. Rather than set one's leading to set two, which leads to set three, which leads to set four, either set three mediates the opposition between set one and set two or set one is to set two as set three is to set four.

The structural meaning of a myth is both non-cumulative and interlocking. It is non-cumulative because the myth contains a series of resolutions of the oppositions it expresses rather than a single, gradual resolution. Every three or four sets provide a resolution, and in either of the fashions described, but the myth as a whole does not. Its meaning is thus cyclical rather than linear, recurrent rather than progressive. Each cycle of three or four sets, like each cycle of the three or four elements within a set, represents not the consequence but only the 'transformation', or variant expression, of its predecessor.

The structural meaning of a myth is interlocking because the meaning of any element within a set lies not in itself but in its 'dialectical' relationship to other elements in the set. Similarly, the meaning of any set lies not in itself but in its 'dialectical' relationship to other sets. By itself, an element or a set has no meaning, literal or symbolic.

A myth has the same interlocking and non-cumulative relationship to other myths as its parts have to one another. Its meaning lies not in itself but in its 'dialectical' relationship to other myths, and the set composed of these myths represents the 'transformation' rather than the consequence of its predecessor. Finally, myths collectively have the same relationship to other human phenomena, including rituals, as individual myths have to one another. In Lévi-Strauss' unique brand of myth-ritualism, myths and rituals operate together, but as structural opposites rather than, as for other myth-ritualists, parallels.

Vladimir Propp, Georges Dumézil, and the Gernet School

Lévi-Strauss is not the only or even the earliest theorist of myth labelled a structuralist. Notably, the Russian folklorist Vladimir Propp (1895–1970) and the French Indo-Europeanist Georges Dumézil (1898–1986) wrote both before Lévi-Strauss and independently of him. The common plot that, as summarized in Chapter 5 on myth and literature, Propp deciphers in Russian fairy tales is his structure. Unlike that of Lévi-Strauss, who disdains his effort for this reason, Propp's structure remains on the narrative level and is therefore no different from the kind of 'structure' found by Otto Rank, Joseph Campbell, or Lord Raglan. By contrast, the structure that Dumézil unravels lies no less beneath the surface level than Lévi-Strauss', but it reflects the order of society rather than, as for Lévi-Strauss, the order of the mind, and is three-part rather than two-part. His theory will be considered in Chapter 8.

A group of French classicists inspired by Louis Gernet and headed by Jean-Pierre Vernant (1914–2007) have proved the most faithful followers of Lévi-Strauss' brand of structuralism, though even they have altered it. Lévi-Strauss has regularly been lambasted for isolating myth from its various contexts—social, cultural, political, economic, even sexual. True, in his essay on Asdiwal he does provide a detailed ethnographic analysis of a myth, examining and integrating geographical, economic, sociological, and cosmological factors. But he does so almost nowhere else. Vernant and his fellow classicists—notably, Marcel Detienne, Pierre Vidal-Naquet, and Nicole Loraux—have taken the analysis of Asdiwal as their model. As the heirs of Lévi-Strauss, these classicists have sought to decipher underlying, often latent patterns in myths, but they have then sought to link those patterns to ones in the culture at large.

Marcel Detienne on Adonis

The French classicist Marcel Detienne (b. 1935), at the time a committed disciple of Lévi-Strauss, devoted a whole book to the myth of Adonis: *The Gardens of Adonis*. Where for Frazer Adonis is an impersonal force rather than a god, for Detienne Adonis is a human being rather than a god. Where for Frazer Adonis symbolizes vegetation, for Detienne one form of vegetation symbolizes—better, parallels—Adonis. Where for Frazer Adonis, like vegetation, annually dies and revives, for Detienne Adonis, like the vegetation associated with him, grows up quickly and then just as quickly dies, once and for all. Above all, where for Frazer the meaning of the myth lies in the plot—the birth, adolescence, death, and rebirth of Adonis—for Detienne the meaning lies in the dialectical relationship among the elements of the plot— characters, places, times, and events.

For Detienne, following Lévi-Strauss, this dialectical relationship exists on a host of levels: dietary, botanical, astronomical, seasonal, religious, and social. At each level a middle ground lies between extremes. The levels parallel one another rather than, like the conscious and unconscious levels of myth for Freud and Jung, symbolize one another. The relationship among the elements at, say, the dietary level is similar to that at the botanical. Still, the dietary level—with cereals and cooked meat lying between spices at one extreme and lettuce and raw meat at the other—most tightly links the others.

Detienne first associates spices with the gods, cereals and cooked meat with humans, and lettuce and raw meat with animals. Spices are burned during sacrifices to the gods. The smell ascends to the gods, who inhale it as the equivalent of food. Because the meat is cooked rather than burned, it goes to humans, who also cultivate cereals. Just as burned meat goes to the gods in the form of fumes, so raw meat goes to animals, with which Detienne also somehow links lettuce. Spices are further associated with the gods because of their relationship to the sun and so, as the place atop earth in the Greek imagination, to Olympus. Spices not only are burned by the sun but also grow where and when the sun is nearest: in the hottest places and on the hottest days of summer. By contrast, lettuce is cold and is therefore connected with the coldest places and times: the world below earth—the seas and the Underworld— and winter. To eat meat raw is to eat it 'cold'.

Cereals and cooked meat lie between spices on the one hand and lettuce and raw meat on the other. Just as, for humans, meat must be cooked rather than either burned or eaten raw, so cereals, to grow, need some sun but not too much. Cereals are therefore grown neither above ground nor below it but in it. Where spices are gathered during the summer and lettuce somehow during the winter, crops are harvested in the autumn in between.

Spices are tied to the gods for other reasons. Less cultivated than gathered, they require no work and thereby befit the lives of the gods. Conversely, animals, eating only what they find, do not work for their supper either. But the gods eat what they want. Animals eat only what they find. The gods, then, do not have to work to eat better than humans. Animals, by not working, eat worse than humans. Humans again fall in between. They must work to eat, but when they work, they have enough, if barely enough, to eat. In the Greek poet Hesiod's Golden Age, humans were like the gods precisely because they had plenty without working. In the future they will be like animals, refusing to work and so presumably going hungry.

Spices are associated not only with gods but also with promiscuity. Rather than making promiscuity a divine prerogative, Detienne deems Zeus and Hera the perfect couple, even in the face of Zeus' escapades. Not gods but spices, with their fragrant, hence seductive, aroma, are connected to promiscuity. Not coincidentally, spices pervaded the Adonia festival, which was celebrated during the hottest days and which was notorious for its promiscuity. Conversely, Detienne links not animals but lettuce and raw meat to sterility and celibacy. For the foul smell of at least rotten, if not raw, meat—Detienne somehow equates the two— repels rather than attracts and thereby fends off sex. Not coincidentally, the women of Lemnos were spurned by men because of their stench.

Between promiscuity on the one hand and sterility or celibacy on the other stands marriage, with which, notes Detienne, the Thesmophoria festival was connected. Though barred to men, the festival, which was celebrated annually at Athens for three days, really celebrated marriage. If its celebrants were all female, they were also all married. Falling between the fragrance of the Adonia and the stench of Lemnos, the mildly foul smell of the festival served to fend off men during only the festival.

Detienne connects all of these levels with the life of Adonis and with the ritualistic gardens dedicated to him. At every level, argues Detienne, Adonis falls in either extreme rather than in the middle. Indeed, Adonis jumps from one extreme to the other, bypassing the middle. Adonis' fate represents that of any human who dares to act like a god: he is reduced to an animal. Daring to be promiscuous, he proves impotent.

For Detienne, as a structuralist, the extremes on each level *parallel*, not *symbolize*, the life of Adonis. At each level the extremes are to the middle as Adonis is to normal humans. Where for Frazer the myth uses humans to symbolize impersonal forces of nature, for Detienne the myth uses impersonal forces of nature as analogues to human behaviour.

The gardens of Adonis, planted during the Adonia festival, involve little work. The plants shoot up immediately. Tending them parallels the toilless lives of the gods. In fact, the gardens are like the spices of the gods. The plants are merely gathered, not cultivated, and grow in the hottest places and times. They are carried to the roofs of houses at the height of summer. Where regular crops take eight months to grow, the plants take only eight days. Where regular crops demand the strength of men, the gardens are tended by women. Unlike the spices, however, the gardens die as quickly as they sprout; and unlike regular crops, they die without yielding food. Having begun above the earth, they end up below it—cast into the sea. In short, the gardens are a futile 'get rich quick' scheme to get food without work. Gods need not work, but humans must. When they seek 'fast food' instead of regular fare, they get no food at all.

Adonis himself is related to spices through his mother, Myrrha, who becomes a myrrh tree. Adonis' gestation takes place in the tree, and his birth requires his breaking out of it. In Ovid's version wood nymphs even bathe the infant in the myrrh formed from his mother's tears. More important, Adonis is tied to spices through promiscuity. Unable to control her desire, Adonis' mother commits incest with her father. Unable to control their desire, Aphrodite and Persephone, according to Apollodorus, fight for custody of the infant Adonis. Adonis himself, for

Detienne, is less an innocent victim of divine seduction than a seducer of divinities.

Adonis is a precocious seducer. Like the gardens, he grows up quickly. But like the gardens as well, he dies quickly. Just as the gardens die too early to yield any food, so Adonis dies too young to marry and have children. Having begun promiscuous, he ends up sterile. Conversely, his mother, who began sterile or at least abstinent—she had spurned all males—becomes promiscuous, to say the least. Jumping from one extreme to the other, mother and son alike reject and, more, threaten the middle ground of marriage.

Adonis' sterility takes the form of not only childlessness but also effeminacy. His death from the boar shows his unfitness for the masculine hunt. Instead of the hunter, he becomes the hunted. His effeminacy signifies insufficient distance between male and female. His mother's initial rejection of all males signifies the opposite. The ideal lies, again, in between: males and females should be related but distinct.

Just as Detienne links Adonis' promiscuity with spices, so he links Adonis' sterility and death with lettuce, in which, in several variants of the myth, Adonis tries vainly to hide from the boar. Myrrh causes sexual arousal; lettuce, sterility or impotence.

Put summarily, Adonis does not know his place. He does not know that he is neither god nor animal but human and that what is distinctively human is marriage. In dying before marrying, he fails to fulfil his human nature.

If the *meaning* of the myth for Detienne is the presentation of an almost endless series of levels, the *function* of the myth is social. It advocates marriage as the middle ground between promiscuity on the one hand and sterility or celibacy on the other—and also, as Chapter 8 will consider, a bulwark of the *polis*.

Chapter 8
Myth and politics

Some theories see myth as political, others do not. Because myth for Tylor and Frazer is about the physical rather than the social world, it is hard to find any political element in myth for them. Yet Frazer, at least, cynically parallels intellectual change to political change. Magicians become kings and 'gradually rise to wealth and power'. Priests succeed magicians and themselves become kings, initially merely human but eventually divine, and 'no class of the community has benefited so much as kings by this belief in the possible incarnation of a god in human form'. Frazer even writes of 'the great social revolution which thus begins with democracy and ends in despotism'.

Bronislaw Malinowski

For Bronislaw Malinowski, myth deals with social phenomena— marriage, taxes, and, as already considered in Chapter 4, ritual—as much as with physical ones—flooding, disease, and death. Myth still serves to reconcile humans to the impositions of life, but now to impositions that, unlike physical ones, *can* be cast off. Here, too, myths spur resigned acceptance by tracing these impositions back to a hoary past. The past confers on them the clout of tradition:

> The myth comes into play when rite, ceremony, or a social or moral rule demands justification, warrant of antiquity, reality, and sanctity.

Myth persuades denizens to defer to, say, ranks in society by pronouncing those ranks long-standing and in that sense deserved. A myth about the British monarchy would make the institution as ancient as possible, so that to tamper with it would be to tamper with tradition. Until recently, fox hunting in England was legal—defended on the grounds that it had long been part of country life. In the case of physical phenomena the beneficiary of myth is the individual. In the case of social phenomena the beneficiary is society itself.

To say that myth traces back the origin of phenomena is equivalent to saying that myth explains those phenomena. When, then, Malinowski, railing against theorists like Tylor, decries the 'present-day mythological opinion' that there exists 'the etiological myth, corresponding to a non-existent desire to explain', he is really asserting that myths are not explanations for their own sake. Yet explanations they must still be, for only by explaining phenomena do they serve their conciliatory function.

Malinowski never makes clear whether moderns as well as primitives have myths. As modern science provides far more control over the physical world than primitive science does, there are surely fewer modern myths of physical phenomena. If there are none, there can still be modern myths of social phenomena. If not even these remain, their place has been taken by ideology.

Georges Sorel

The view of myth as itself ideology is to be found classically in *Reflections on Violence*, by the French syndicalist Georges Sorel (1847–1922). For Sorel, myth is eternal, not merely primitive, and, antithetically to Malinowski, serves not to bolster society but to topple it. Sorel asserts that the only way to establish the socialist ideal is through revolution, which requires both violence and myth. By 'violence' he means forceful action but not mere bloodshed. The key 'violent' action is a strike by all workers. By 'myth' he means a guiding ideology, one that preaches an imminent end to present society, advocates a fight to the death with the ruling class, makes rebels heroes, declares the certainty of victory, and espouses a moral standard for the future society:

> In the course of this study one thing has always been present in my mind...that men who are participating in a great social movement always picture their coming action as a battle in which their cause is certain to triumph. These constructions...I propose to call myths; the syndicalist 'general strike' and Marx's catastrophic revolution are such myths.

Oliver Cromwell's conviction that God had ordained him to remove King Charles I of England and transform society would typify myth for Sorel.

Sorel asserts that both violence and myth are indispensable for revolution and are therefore justified. He spurns any neutral, scientific analysis of myth, including a Marxist one. He turns Marxism itself into a myth, for commitment to it goads followers to revolution. Sorel is like Malinowski in his indifference to the truth of myth. For both, what matters is that myth works when believed to be true. And for Sorel, the ultimate truth of myth—the success of a revolution—is in any case unknowable in advance.

For Malinowski, myth is like ideology in justifying submission to society. For Sorel, myth *is* ideology in justifying rejection of society. Sorel's theory is wholly inapplicable to the case of Adonis, who acts alone, is more passive victim than active agent, and is hardly motivated by any ideology. Sorel's theory clearly fits today's terrorists, whose myth justifies 9/11 as the first stage in the defeat of the demonic West. Sorel enlists the term myth to underscore the grip of an ideology.

Ernst Cassirer

Ernst Cassirer came to see myth as not merely primitive but also modern. Fleeing to America from Hitler's Germany, he came to focus on modern political myths, above all those of Nazism. Myth here amounts to ideology. Having previously concentrated on ethereal, philosophical issues, Cassirer now turns to brute, social scientific ones: how do political myths take and keep hold? Having previously scorned Lévy-Bruhl's supposed stress on the irrationality of myth, Cassirer now embraces it:

> In all critical moments of man's social life, the rational forces that resist the rise of the old mythical conceptions are no longer sure of themselves. In these moments the time for myth has come again.

Tying myth to magic and magic to a desperate effort to control the social world, Cassirer applies to *modern* myths the explication of *primitive* myths by Malinowski, whom he cites. Indeed, he sees modern myths as an atavistic revival of primitivism.

Where previously Cassirer analysed myth as quasi-philosophy, now he cuts off myth from philosophy. Myth now is anything but a form of knowledge with a distinctive logic to be teased out. The marginalized role left philosophy is to challenge political myths:

> It is beyond the power of philosophy to destroy the political myths. A myth is in a sense invulnerable. It is impervious to rational arguments; it cannot be refuted by syllogisms. But philosophy can do us another important service. It can make us understand the adversary.... We should carefully study the origin, the structure, the methods, and the technique of the political myths. We should see the adversary face to face in order to know how to combat him.

It is hard to see how this proposed study of political myths is really a task for philosophy rather than for social science. Myth is now

Myth and politics

115

not merely prelogical but outright illogical—a position far more extreme than that for which Cassirer castigates Lévy-Bruhl!

Dumézil

Georges Dumézil, mentioned in Chapter 7 as a structuralist, might be considered as other than a theorist of myth because he confines himself to Indo-European mythology rather than to myths generally. More, he insists on the uniqueness of this domain. Still, the huge area he covers encompasses many cultures, and others have tried to extend his theory to yet other areas.

Dumézil derives Indo-European religions and in turn myths and gods from social structure, which is the base of Indo-European society. Dumézil is at heart a sociologist. Like Plato in the *Republic*, he divides Indo-European society into three classes: at the top the priests, in the middle the warriors, and at the bottom the herders and farmers. Unlike Plato, he does not root this structure in the cosmos but roots it instead in society. Each class, or 'stratum', had its distinctive 'function'. By 'function' Dumézil means the way in which a class does its job. Each class has its own myths and gods, and they reflect the function of that class. Together, the three classes constitute what he calls the Indo-European 'ideology'. Myth serves not to justify that structure but to express it.

Critics of Dumézil have suggested that his argument for a distinctive Indo-European ideology is also an endorsement of it and, more, that his characterization of this ancient ideology matches that of modern Fascism. Dumézil, himself French, began writing at the time that Fascism in Italy and Germany was starting to peak. In *Ayran Idols* Stefan Arvidsson sums up the charge:

> Dumézil's work amounted to an attempt to confer historical background and legitimacy on the Fascist dream of a society

that would be harmoniously integrated and, at the same time, hierarchically divided into leaders, soldiers, and workers. By implying that the prehistoric Indo-Europeans had structured their society and their worldview according to a hierarchical tripartite pattern, Dumézil wanted to make the Fascist ideals appear natural.

Dumézil does use 'Aryan' interchangeably with Indo-European and does pit the Indo-European outlook against the liberal outlook of Judaism and Christianity.

More common than regional myths are myths of nations. Many nations espouse stories that make them God's chosen. The wars and conquests of those nations are justified by myths. At sports events, national anthems that tie the nation to God are sung. The United States has long seen itself as a new Eden, thereby invoking Genesis 3. Israel derives itself from the promise made by God to Abraham in Genesis 12.

René Girard

René Girard, whose take on Frazer's myth-ritualism was considered in Chapter 5, transforms not merely the relationship between myth and ritual but also the origin and function of both. The two arise to secure not food but peace. The scapegoat, whether king or commoner, is sacrificed to end not winter but violence, which is the *problem* rather than, as for Sorel, the *solution*. Myth and ritual are ways of coping not with nature but with human nature—with human aggression.

In *Violence and the Sacred* Girard, like Raglan and Rank, cites Oedipus as the best example of his theory. Far from causing the plague besetting Thebes during his reign as king, Oedipus, according to Girard, is in fact an innocent victim. Either there never was a plague, or the plague was not the cause of the upheaval. Or the plague is a metaphor for violence, which has spread across society like a contagion. The violence among

Thebans is evinced in the tension among the principals of Sophocles' play: Oedipus, Creon, and Teiresias.

The only way to end the violence is by making a scapegoat of a vulnerable member of society. Even though he is king, Oedipus is doubly stigmatized and thereby doubly vulnerable. He is an outsider: he is not yet known to be a Theban and has won the throne not by heredity but by the toppling of the Sphinx. And he is a cripple—the result of the piercing of his ankles at birth. The myth, concocted only after Oedipus' downfall, serves to absolve the community by blaming him: he has killed his father and married his mother, and it is for his parricide and his incest that Thebes now endures plague. Or so argues Sophocles' Teiresias.

In actuality, according to Girard, the Thebans simply decide to accept Teiresias' and Creon's opinions rather than Oedipus' opinion over who is responsible for the breakdown in society. Only the subsequent myth turns the victors' opinions into the truth:

> The Thebans—religious believers—sought a cure for their ills in a formal acceptance of the myth, in making it the indisputable version of the events that had recently convulsed the city and in making it the charter for a new cultural order—by convincing themselves, in short, that all their miseries were due exclusively to the plague. Such an attitude requires absolute faith in the guilt of the surrogate victim.

That collective violence rather than the lone Oedipus is the real cause of the problem is borne out by events thereafter. True, the plague ends, but it is soon followed by a fight for the throne among Creon, Oedipus' son Polynices, and his other son, Eteocles. According to Girard, Sophocles challenges the myth, but never explicitly, so that the play has regularly been taken, by Harrison and Murray included, as the dramatized *version* of the myth rather than as, for the professedly more perceptive Girard, a *challenge* to the myth.

But the myth, which continues with *Oedipus at Colonus*, does more than blame Oedipus for Theban woes. It proceeds to turn him into a hero. Even as king, Oedipus is heroic in deeming it his duty to end the plague that has befallen his subjects, in vowing to discover who the culprit is, and in insisting on being banished once he discovers that he himself is the culprit. Yet for Girard the real hero is not the fallen, self-sacrificing Oedipus, as for Raglan, but the elevated one. Even as culprit, Oedipus has the power to save Thebes: just as his presence caused the plague, so his departure ends it. He is a hero even while a criminal. He already has the god-like power both to bring plague and to end it.

But by the time of *Oedipus at Colonus* Oedipus' stature has grown. Having arrived, after years of wandering, at Colonus, near Athens, he is now ordered to return to Thebes. Just as the welfare of Thebes once depended on Oedipus' exile, now it depends on his return. Oedipus refuses, for we learn that he had wanted to remain at Thebes following the events in *Oedipus the King* but had eventually been forcibly exiled by Creon and others. Now Creon is prepared to seize him and bring him back to Thebes. King Theseus offers Oedipus asylum. In return, Oedipus declares that his burial spot in Athens will protect Athens against Thebes. In short, Oedipus, having in *Oedipus the King* begun as a divine-like King of Thebes, in *Oedipus at Colonus* ends as a divine-like benefactor of Athens.

Adonis

Ancient Greeks linked psychological immaturity to political immaturity: Adonis' failure to become an adult would have meant his failure to become a citizen. Adonis would have been suited for precisely that form of government which involves no responsibility and assumes political infancy: tyranny. Adonis' submission to mother-like gods fits a matriarchal society. Having experienced only smothering females, he projects those qualities onto all females and thereby submits unquestioningly to them.

The family constitutes the link between personality and the *polis*, the city-state run by male citizens. The opposition that Herodotus draws between the *polis* of Greece, in which even the ruler is subject to the law, and the tyranny of the East, in which the ruler is above the law, holds for family life as well.

Adonis is incapable of citizenship because he, like the tyrants, is incapable of family life. On the one hand he fosters no family: he never marries, has no children, and dies young. On the other hand he is born into no family: he is the child of incest, not marriage, and his father tries to kill his mother. He is thus doubly barred from citizenship: he lacks not only maturity but also a pedigree, itself the result of the immaturity of his mother. If Herodotus testifies to the political necessity of siring a family, the Aristotelian *Constitution of the Athenians* testifies to the political necessity of descending from one: 'the right of citizenship belongs to those whose parents have been citizens'.

The Greeks linked immaturity not only to politics but also to hunting. Adonis' haplessness at hunting would have symbolized his haplessness at adulthood. He becomes the hunted instead of the hunter. He has no conception of hunting and of its dangers. Either he thinks the world maternal, or he thinks himself protected from it by maternal goddesses. To Venus' warnings that dangerous animals respect neither youth nor beauty, he is deaf.

The tie between human and hunter becomes a metaphor for the tie between human and citizen. Pierre Vidal-Naquet (1930–2006) suggests that hunting was a key aspect of the two-year military stint that, according to the *Constitution of the Athenians*, Athenian youths were required to undergo before citizenship. Vidal-Naquet argues that these adolescent youths, or *ephebes*, engaged in a brand of hunting that was the opposite of the brand that, as adult *hoplites*, they would soon be undertaking. As *ephebes*, they hunted individually, in the mountains, at night, and armed only with nets—thereby relying on trickery to capture their prey. As *hoplites*, they would be hunting in a group, on the plain, during the day, and armed with spears—thus relying on courage and skill to kill their prey.

Vidal-Naquet names two mythic *ephebes* who never become *hoplites*: Melanthos and Melanion. Both succeed at hunting of only an adolescent variety. But Adonis fails at hunting of any kind. He is thus not, like Melanthos and Melanion, merely an adolescent who never advances to adulthood but an infant who never even advances to childhood.

Conclusion: bringing myth back to the world

Nineteenth-century theories of myth, as typified by those of Tylor and Frazer, saw myth as entirely about the physical world. Myth was assumed to be part of religion, which was assumed to be the primitive counterpart to science, which in turn was assumed to be almost entirely modern. In the 20th century Tylor's and Frazer's theories were spurned exactly for pitting myth against science and thereby precluding traditional myths, for subsuming myth under religion and thereby precluding secular myths, for deeming the subject matter of myth the physical world, for deeming the function of myth explanatory, and for deeming myth false.

The overarching contemporary rejoinder to Tylor and Frazer has been the denial that myth must go when science comes. Theories since then have defiantly sought to preserve myth in the face of science. Yet they have not done so by challenging science as the reigning explanation of the physical world. They have not taken any of the easy routes: 'relativizing' science, 'sociologizing' science, 'feminizing' science, or 'mythicizing' science. Rather than re-characterizing science, they have re-characterized myth. Either myth, while still about the world, is not or not just an explanation, in which case its function differs from that of science (Malinowski, Eliade), or myth, read symbolically, is not even about the physical world (Bultmann, Jonas, Camus). Or both (Freud, Rank, Jung,

Campbell). Only with the emergence of postmodernism has the deference to science been questioned.

In so far as present-day theories have not challenged the supremacy of science, why bother trying to reconcile myth with science? Why not simply accept the 19th-century view and dispense with myth in favour of science? The present-day answer has been that the restriction of myth to either a literal explanation (Tylor) or a symbolic description (Frazer) of physical events fails to account for the array of other *functions* and *meanings* that myth harbours. The tell-tale evidence of these other functions and meanings is that myth is still around. If Tylor and Frazer were right, myth would by now be long dead.

In the 21st century the question is whether myth can be brought back to the physical world, but without facilely dismissing the authority of science.

The myth of Gaia

The figures who created the concept of earth as a self-regulating system were scientists: the 18th-century Scottish geologist James Hutton and, much more, the present-day multi-disciplinary English scientist James Lovelock, who was born in 1919 and who, even more than the earth, is still going strong. Both propose the concept as outright scientific and not just as compatible with science. The novelist William Golding suggested to Lovelock the name 'Gaia'.

Gaia, or earth, is the Greek name for one of the first four gods in Hesiod's *Theogony*, the Greek counterpart to the Genesis creation myths. In the *Theogony*, in contrast to Genesis, gods come into existence rather than are presupposed. Hence the title of the work: the 'genesis of gods'. In Genesis God is separate from the world he creates: he creates by himself but not out of himself. In the *Theogony* gods are identical with the forces of nature they control. But soon after the creation the first four gods—Chaos, Gaia, Tartarus, and Eros—become full-fledged personalities. Gaia becomes a thinking, deliberative figure, even if not physically separate from the earth. One can, then, characterize her as a god.

Having noted the contrast between the absence of life on Mars and the presence of life on earth, Lovelock, beginning with his book *Gaia*, maintains that 'the only feasible explanation of the Earth's highly improbable atmosphere was that it was being manipulated on a day-to-day basis from the surface, and that the manipulator was life itself'. In other words, the earth, unlike Mars, regulates itself. The earth not only is designed but is its own designer:

> What are we to make of volcanic activity and continental drift? Both are consequences of the inner motions of our planet, but could Gaia also be at work?
>
> If Gaia has modified the sea floor, it has been done by exploiting a natural tendency and turning it to her own advantage.

The Gaia hypothesis is 'an alternative to that equally depressing picture of our planet as a demented spaceship, forever travelling, driverless and purposeless, around an inner circle of the sun'. If the earth is neither driverless nor purposeless, then it designs itself and is thereby a personality, or a god. Stories of its 'life' are myths.

Yet Lovelock comes to assert that he has been misunderstood:

> the self-regulation of climate and chemical composition [by the earth] are entirely automatic. Self-regulation emerges as the system evolves. No foresight, planning, or teleology (suggestion of designer or purpose in nature) is involved.
>
> You will notice I am continuing to use the metaphor of the 'living Earth' for Gaia; but do not assume that I am thinking of the Earth

as alive in a sentient way, or even alive like an animal or a bacterium.

While myths need not be about gods—they can also be about humans and animals—myths of the physical world must be about gods. While gods need not be identical with the physical world, the way Gaia initially is for Hesiod, they must at least control parts of the physical world. They need not have a plan, the way Lovelock originally assumed, but they must have intent. They must be personalities.

If subsequently for Lovelock the earth is not a personality, then it is not a god, and stories about the earth are not myths. The Gaia hypothesis does not, then, bring myth back to the world.

Lovelock wants to reconcile myth with science. But when challenged, he discards the myth to save the science. The choices for theorists of myth thereby remain those of either the 19th century or the 20th century.

Lovelock cares about the earth. He believes that humans have a responsibility for it—a view that goes back to Genesis 1, in which humans are given 'dominion' over the earth. Lovelock uses the metaphor of a personified earth to garner concern. But the Gaia hypothesis, which he comes to call a 'theory,' is far more. It is about the ability of the earth to save itself, and to do so intentionally.

References and further reading

References are presented in the order in which they appear in each chapter.

Introduction

On the antiquity of theories of myth, see Richard Chase, *Quest for Myth* (Baton Rouge: Louisiana State University Press, 1949), chapter 1; Jan de Vries, *Forschungsgeschichte der Mythologie* (Freiburg: Alber, 1961), chapter 1.

On parallels between earlier theories and social scientific ones, see Burton Feldman and Robert D. Richardson, *The Rise of Modern Mythology, 1680-1860* (Bloomington: Indiana University Press, 1972), pp. xxii-xxiii.

For a standard folkloristic classification of stories, see William Bascom, 'The Forms of Folklore: Prose Narratives', *Journal of American Folklore*, 78 (1965): 3-20. On the blurriness of these distinctions, see Stith Thompson, *The Folktale* (Berkeley: University of California Press, 1977 [1946]), p. 303.

William D. Rubinstein, *The Myth of Rescue: Why the Democracies Could Not Have Saved More Jews from the Nazis* (London and New York: Routledge, 1987).

Wilfrid Sellars, 'Empiricism and the Philosophy of Mind.' In Herbert Feigl and Michael Scriven, eds., *Minnesota Studies in the Philosophy of Science*, vol. I (Minneapolis: University of Minnesota Press, 1956), 253-329.

Apollodorus, *Gods and Heroes of the Greeks: The 'Library' of Apollodorus*, tr. Michael Simpson (Amherst: University of

Massachusetts Press, 1976); Ovid, *Metamorphoses*, tr. Rolfe
Humphries (Bloomington: Indiana University Press, 1955).

For scepticism over the universality of theories, see Stith Thompson,
'Myths and Folktales', *Journal of American Folklore*, 68 (1955):
482–8; G. S. Kirk, *Myth* (Berkeley: University of California Press,
1970), p. 7.

Chapter 1: Myth and science

On the history of creationism, see Ronald L. Numbers, *The
Creationists*, expanded edn. (Cambridge, MA: Harvard University
Press, 2006 [1st edn. 1992]).

On scientific reinterpretation of the Noah myth, see, for example,
William Ryan and Walter Pitman, *Noah's Flood* (London: Simon
and Schuster, 1999). On the array of interpretations of flood stories
worldwide, see Alan Dundes, ed., *The Flood Myth* (Berkeley:
University of California Press, 1988).

In the passage on the plagues of Egypt, the reference is to Herbert G.
May and Bruce M. Metzger, eds., *The New Oxford Annotated Bible
with the Apocrypha*, Revised Standard Version (New York: Oxford
University Press, 1977 [1962]). Quotations are taken from p. 75.
For a comparable attempt to 'naturalize' myth from outside of the
Bible, see Samuel Noah Kramer, *Sumerian Mythology*, rev. edn.
(New York: Harper & Row, 1961 [1st edn. 1944]).

The classic attempt not to replace but to reconcile a theological
account of the plagues with a scientific account is that of the
Jewish existentialist philosopher Martin Buber, for whom the
believer, on the basis of faith, attributes to divine intervention what
the believer acknowledges can be fully accounted for scientifically.
See Buber, *Moses* (New York: Harper Torchbooks, 1958 [1946]),
especially pp. 60–8, 74–9. Buber is the Jewish counterpart to
Rudolf Bultmann, considered in Chapter 2.

The classic work on finding science in myth is Giorgio de Santillana
and Hertha von Dechend, *Hamlet's Mill* (Boston: Gambit, 1969).

The work cited is Andrew Dixon White, *A History of the Warfare of
Science with Theology in Christendom* (1896), abridged by Bruce
Mazlish (New York: Free Press, 1965). For a balanced corrective,
see John Hedley Brooke, *Science and Religion* (Cambridge:
Cambridge University Press, 1991).

The classic work by E. B. Tylor is *Primitive Culture*, 2 vols, 1st edn.
(London: Murray, 1871). Citations are from the reprint of the 5th

(1913) edition (New York: Harper Torchbooks, 1958). The work by Stephen Jay Gould quoted is *Rocks of Ages* (London: Vintage, 2002 [1999]).

For a refreshingly sensible postmodern approach to myth, see Laurence Coupe, *Myth*, 2nd edn. (London and New York: Routledge, 2009 [1st edn. 1997]).

For a modern Tylorian perspective, see David Bidney, *Theoretical Anthropology*, 2nd edn. (New York: Schocken, 1967 [1st edn. 1953]), chapter 10; 'Myth, Symbolism, and Truth', *Journal of American Folklore*, 68 (1955): 379–92.

On the term 'euhemerist', see Joseph Fontenrose, *The Ritual Theory of Myth* (Berkeley: University of California Press, 1966), pp. 20–3.

Friedrich Max Müller, 'Comparative Mythology' (1856), in his *Chips from a German Workshop* (London: Longmans, Green, 1867), pp. 1–141.

A theologian who assumes that Genesis 1 is anything but an account of creation is Langdon Gilkey. See his *Maker of Heaven and Earth* (Lanham, MD: University Press of America, 1985 [1959]), especially pp. 25–9, 148–55.

J. G. Frazer, *The Golden Bough*, 1st edn., 2 vols (London: Macmillan, 1890); 2nd edn., 3 vols (London: Macmillan, 1900); 3rd edn., 12 vols (London: Macmillan, 1911–15); one-vol. abridgment (London: Macmillan, 1922).

Lucien Lévy-Bruhl, *How Natives Think*, tr. Lilian A. Clare (New York: Washington Square Press, 1966 [1926]).

Bronislaw Malinowski, 'Magic, Science and Religion' (1925) and 'Myth in Primitive Psychology' (1926), in his *Magic, Science and Religion and Other Essays*, ed. Robert Redfield (Garden City, NY: Doubleday Anchor Books, 1954 [1948]), pp. 17–92 and 93–148.

Claude Lévi-Strauss, *The Savage Mind*, tr. not given (Chicago: University of Chicago Press, 1966); *Myth and Meaning* (Toronto: University of Toronto Press, 1978); André Akoun et al., 'A Conversation with Claude Lévi-Strauss', *Psychology Today*, 5 (May 1972): 36–9, 74–82.

Karl Popper, *Conjectures and Refutations*, 5th edn. (London: Routledge & Kegan Paul, 1974 [1st edn. 1962]); *The World of Parmenides*, eds. Arne F. Peterson and Jorgen Mejer (London: Routledge, 1998); *The Myth of the Framework*, ed. M. A. Notturno (London and New York: Routledge, 1994).

F. M. Cornford, *From Religion to Philosophy* (London: Arnold, 1912); *Principium Sapientiae*, ed. W. K. C. Guthrie (Cambridge: Cambridge University Press, 1952), chapters 1–11.

Chapter 2: Myth and philosophy

Paul Radin, *Primitive Man as Philosopher*, 2nd edn. (New York: Dover, 1957 [1st edn. 1927]); *The World of Primitive Man* (New York: Dutton, 1971), chapter 3.

Ernst Cassirer, *The Philosophy of Symbolic Forms*, tr. Ralph Manheim, II (New Haven, CT: Yale University Press, 1955).

The fullest application to philosophy of Lévy-Bruhl and Cassirer is to be found in Henri Frankfort, H. A. Frankfort, John A. Wilson, Thorkild Jacobsen, and William A. Irwin, *The Intellectual Adventure of Ancient Man: An Essay on Speculative Thought in the Ancient Near East* (Chicago: University of Chicago Press, 1946 [reprinted Phoenix Books, 1997]); paperback retitled *Before Philosophy: The Intellectual Adventure of Ancient Man: An Essay on Speculative Thought in the Ancient Near East* (Harmondsworth: Pelican Books, 1949).

Rudolf Bultmann, 'New Testament and Mythology' (1941), in *Kerygma and Myth*, ed. Hans-Werner Bartsch, tr. Reginald H. Fuller, I (London: SPCK, 1953), pp. 1–44; *Jesus Christ and Mythology* (New York: Scribner's, 1958); Hans Jonas, *Gnosis und spätantiker Geist*, 2 vols, 1st edn. (Göttingen: Vandenhoeck und Ruprecht, 1934 [vol. I] and 1954 [vol. II, part 1]); *The Gnostic Religion*, 2nd edn. (Boston: Beacon Press, 1963 [1958]), Epilogue.

For the myth of Sisyphus, see Albert Camus, *The Myth of Sisyphus and Other Essays*, tr. Justin O'Brien (New York: Vintage Books, 1960 [1955]), pp. 88–91; Homer, *The Odyssey*, tr. Richmond Lattimore (New York: Harper Torchbooks, 1968 [1965]), p. 183.

Chapter 3: Myth and religion

Bultmann, 'New Testament and Mythology' and *Jesus Christ and Mythology*.

For Jaspers' debate with Bultmann, see Karl Jaspers and Rudolf Bultmann, *Myth and Christianity*, tr. Norman Guterman (New York: Noonday Press, 1958).

Jonas, *The Gnostic Religion*.

Jonas is not the only philosopher to 'update' Gnosticism. The political philosopher Eric Voegelin seeks to show how modern movements like positivism, Marxism, Communism, Fascism, and psychoanalysis evince what he calls 'the Gnostic attitude'. See his *Science, Politics and Gnosticism* (Chicago: Regnery Gateway Editions, 1968) and *The New Science of Politics* (Chicago: University of Chicago Press, 1952).

On Norman Schwarzkopf, see Jack Anderson and Dale Van Atta, *Stormin' Norman: An American Hero* (New York: Zebra Books, 1971).

Mircea Eliade, *Myth and Reality*, tr. Willard R. Trask (New York: Harper Torchbooks, 1968 [1963]); *The Sacred and the Profane*, tr. Willard R. Trask (New York: Harvest Books, 1968 [1959]).

On John F. Kennedy, Jr, see, for example, Wendy Leigh, *Prince Charming* (New York: New American Library, 2000); Christopher Anderson, *The Day John Died* (New York: William Morrow, 2000); Richard Blow, *American Son* (New York: Henry Holt, 2002).

On George Washington, see Barry Schwartz, *George Washington* (New York: Free Press; London: Collier Macmillan, 1987); Mason Weems, *The Life of Washington*, 9th edn., ed. Peter S. Onuf (Armonk, NY: Sharpe, 1996 [1st edn. 1800; 9th edn. 1809]), pp. 9–10.

Chapter 4: Myth and ritual

William Robertson Smith, *Lectures on the Religion of the Semites*, First Series, 1st edn. (Edinburgh: Black, 1889), Lecture 1.

Tylor, *Primitive Culture*, 5th edn., II, chapter 18.

Frazer, *The Golden Bough*, abridged edn., especially chapters 29–33 (first myth-ritualist scenario); 6–8, 24 (second myth-ritualist scenario).

Jane Ellen Harrison, *Themis*, 1st edn. (Cambridge: Cambridge University Press, 1912); *Alpha and Omega* (London: Sidgwick & Jackson, 1915), chapter 6; *Epilegomena to the Study of Greek Religion* (Cambridge: Cambridge University Press, 1921); on myth and art, *Ancient Art and Ritual* (New York: Holt; London: Williams and Norgate, 1913).

S. H. Hooke, 'The Myth and Ritual Pattern of the Ancient East', in *Myth and Ritual*, ed. Hooke (London: Oxford University Press, 1933), chapter 1; Introduction to *The Labyrinth*, ed. Hooke (London: SPCK; New York: Macmillan, 1935), pp. v–x; *The Origins of Early Semitic Ritual* (London: Oxford University Press, 1938); 'Myth and Ritual: Past and Present', in *Myth, Ritual, and Kingship*, ed. Hooke (Oxford: Clarendon Press, 1958), chapter 1.

Gregory Nagy, 'Can Myth Be Saved?', in *Myth*, eds. Gregory Schrempp and William Hansen (Bloomington: Indiana University Press,

2002), chapter 15. See also Edmund Leach, *Political Systems of Highland Burma* (Boston: Beacon, 1965 [1954]); 'Ritualization in Man', *Philosophical Transactions of the Royal Society*, Series B, no. 772, vol. 251 (1966): 403–8.

Gilbert Murray, 'Excursis on the Ritual Forms Preserved in Greek Tragedy', in Harrison, *Themis*, pp. 341–63; *Euripides and His Age*, 1st edn. (New York: Holt; London: Williams and Norgate, 1913), pp. 60–8; *Aeschylus* (Oxford: Clarendon Press, 1940); 'Dis Geniti', *Journal of Hellenic Studies*, 71 (1951): 120–8; on myth and literature, 'Hamlet and Orestes: A Study in Traditional Types', *Proceedings of the British Academy*, 6 (1913–14): 389–412.

F. M. Cornford, 'The Origin of the Olympic Games', in Harrison, *Themis*, chapter 7; *The Origin of Attic Comedy* (London: Arnold, 1914); 'A Ritual Basis for Hesiod's *Theogony*' (1941), in his *The Unwritten Philosophy and Other Essays*, ed. W. K. C. Guthrie (Cambridge: Cambridge University Press, 1950), pp. 95–116; *Principium Sapientiae*, ed. W. K. C. Guthrie (Cambridge: Cambridge University Press, 1952), pp. 191–256.

A. B. Cook, *Zeus*, 3 vols in 5 (Cambridge: Cambridge University Press, 1914–40).

Ivan Engnell, *Studies in Divine Kingship in the Ancient Near East*, 1st edn. (Uppsala: Almqvist & Wiksells, 1943); *A Rigid Scrutiny*, ed. and tr. John T. Willis (Nashville: Vanderbilt University Press, 1969) (retitled *Critical Essays on the Old Testament* [London: SPCK, 1970]).

Aubrey R. Johnson, 'The Role of the King in the Jerusalem Cults', in *The Labyrinth*, ed. Hooke, pp. 73–111; 'Hebrew Conceptions of Kingship', in *Myth, Ritual, and Kingship*, ed. Hooke, pp. 204–35; *Sacral Kingship in Ancient Israel*, 1st edn. (Cardiff: University of Wales Press, 1955).

Sigmund Mowinckel, *The Psalms in Israel's Worship*, tr. D. R. Ap-Thomas, 2 vols (New York: Abingdon, 1962); *He That Cometh*, tr. G. W. Anderson (Nashville: Abingdon, 1954), chapter 3.

Malinowski, 'Myth in Primitive Psychology'; 'Magic, Science and Religion', especially pp. 83–4; 'The Role of Myth in Life', *Psyche*, 6 (1926): 29–39; *Malinowski and the Work of Myth*, ed. Ivan Strenski (Princeton, NJ: Princeton University Press, 1992).

Eliade, *The Sacred and the Profane*, chapter 2; *Myth and Reality*.

Applications of the theory of myth to literature: Jessie L. Weston, *From Ritual to Romance* (Cambridge: Cambridge University Press, 1920); E. M. Butler, *The Myth of the Magus* (Cambridge: Cambridge

University Press; New York: Macmillan, 1948); C. L. Barber, *Shakespeare's Festive Comedy* (Princeton, NJ: Princeton University Press, 1959); Herbert Weisinger, *Tragedy and the Paradox of the Fortunate Fall* (London: Routledge & Kegan Paul; East Lansing: Michigan State College Press, 1953); Francis Fergusson, *The Idea of a Theater* (Princeton, NJ: Princeton University Press, 1949); Lord Raglan, 'Myth and Ritual', *Journal of American Folklore*, 68 (1955): 454–61; Northrop Frye, *Anatomy of Criticism* (Princeton, NJ: Princeton University Press, 1957), pp. 131–239; Stanley Edgar Hyman, 'Myth, Ritual, and Nonsense', *Kenyon Review*, 11 (1949): 455–75.

René Girard, *Violence and the Sacred*, tr. Patrick Gregory (London: Athlone Press; Baltimore: Johns Hopkins University Press, 1977); *'To Double Business Bound'* (London: Athlone Press; Baltimore: Johns Hopkins University Press, 1978); *The Scapegoat*, tr. Yvonne Freccero (London: Athlone Press; Baltimore: Johns Hopkins University Press, 1986); *Things Hidden since the Foundation of the World*, trs. Stephen Bann and Michael Metteer (London: Athlone Press; Stanford, CA: Stanford University Press, 1987); *Job, the Victim of his People*, tr. Yvonne Freccero (London: Athlone Press; Stanford, CA: Stanford University Press, 1987); 'Generative Scapegoating', in *Violent Origins*, ed. Robert G. Hamerton-Kelly (Stanford, CA: Stanford University Press, 1987), pp. 73–105. Against Frazer, see Girard, *Violence and the Sacred*, pp. 28–30, 96, 121–3, 316–18; *The Scapegoat*, p. 120.

Clyde Kluckhohn, 'Myths and Rituals: A General Theory', *Harvard Theological Review*, 35 (1942): 45–79.

Walter Burkert, *Structure and History in Greek Mythology and Ritual* (Berkeley: University of California Press, 1979), especially pp. 56–8, 99–101; *Homo Necans*, tr. Peter Bing (Berkeley: University of California Press, 1983), especially pp. 29–34; *Ancient Mystery Cults* (Cambridge, MA: Harvard University Press, 1987), pp. 73–8; 'The Problem of Ritual Killing', in *Violent Origins*, ed. Hamerton-Kelly, pp. 149–76; *Creation of the Sacred* (Cambridge, MA: Harvard University Press, 1996), chapters 2–3.

Chapter 5: Myth and literature

On the preservation of classical mythology, see, for example, Douglas Bush, *Mythology and the Renaissance Tradition in English Poetry* (Minneapolis: University of Minnesota Press, 1932); *Mythology* and the Romantic Tradition in English Poetry (Cambridge, MA: Harvard University Press, 1937); Gilbert Highet, *The Classical Tradition* (New York: Oxford University Press, 1939): Jean Seznec, *The Survival of the Pagan Gods* (New York: Pantheon Books, 1953 [1940]). For a useful sourcebook on three classical myths, see Geoffrey Miles, ed., *Classical Mythology in English Literature* (London: Routledge, 1999).

On the influence of Frazer, Freud, and Jung on modern literature, see Lionel Trilling, 'On the Teaching of Modern Literature' (1961), reprinted in Trilling, *Beyond Culture* (New York: Viking Press, 1968), pp. 3–30; Lilian Feder, *Ancient Myth in Modern Poetry* (Princeton, NJ: Princeton University Press, 1971); John B. Vickery, *The Literary Impact of 'The Golden Bough'* (Princeton, NJ: Princeton University Press, 1971).

Jessie L. Weston, *From Ritual to Romance*.

Francis Fergusson, *The Idea of a Theater*; ' "Myth" and the Literary Scruple', *Sewanee Review*, 64 (1956): 171–85.

Northrop Frye, 'The Archetypes of Literature' (1951) and 'Myth, Fiction, and Displacement' (1961), in his *Fables of Identity* (New York: Harcourt, Brace, 1963), pp. 7–20 and 21–38; *Anatomy of Criticism* (Princeton, NJ: Princeton University Press, 1957), pp. 131–239; 'Literature and Myth', in *Relations of Literary Study*, ed. James Thorpe (New York: Modern Language Association, 1967), pp. 27–55; 'Symbolism of the Unconscious' (1959) and 'Forming Fours' (1954), in *Northrop Frye on Culture and Literature*, ed. Robert D. Denham (Chicago: University of Chicago Press, 1978), pp. 84–94 and 117–29; 'Myth', *Antaeus* 43 (1981): 64–84.

See, as classical Jungians, Maud Bodkin, *Archetypal Patterns in Literature* (London: Oxford University Press, 1934); Bettina L. Knapp, *A Jungian Approach to Literature* (Carbondale: Southern Illinois University Press, 1984).

See, as archetypal psychologists, James Hillman, *Re-Visioning Psychology* (New York: Harper & Row, 1975); David L. Miller, *The New Polytheism* (Dallas: Spring Publications, 1981).

Girard, *Violence and the Sacred*.

On the terms plot, text, story, and narrative, see Shlomith Rimmon-Kenan, *Narrative Fiction*, 2nd edn. (London and New York: Routledge, 2002 [1st edn. 1983]); Paul Cobley, *Narrative* (London and New York: Routledge, 2001).

Kenneth Burke, *The Rhetoric of Religion* (Boston: Beacon Press, 1961); *A Grammar of Motives* (New York: Prentice-Hall, 1945),

Myth

pp. 430–40; 'Myth, Poetry and Philosophy', *Journal of American Folklore*, 73 (1960): pp. 283–306.

Hans Blumenberg, *Work on Myth*, tr. Robert M. Wallace. (Cambridge, MA: MIT Press, 1985 [1979 in German]).

Tylor, *Primitive Culture*, 5th edn., I, pp. 281–2. Hero myths are a surprising category for someone for whom all myths are seemingly about physical events.

Johann Georg von Hahn, *Sagwissenschaftliche Studien* (Jena: Mauke, 1876), p. 340; tr. Henry Wilson in John C. Dunlop, *History of Prose Fiction*, rev. Wilson (London: Bell, 1888), in an unnumbered attachment to the last page of vol. I.

Vladimir Propp, *Morphology of the Folktale*, tr. Laurence Scott, 2nd edn., rev. and ed. Louis A. Wagner (Austin: University of Texas Press, 1968 [1958]).

Otto Rank, *The Myth of the Birth of the Hero*, 1st edn., trs. F. Robbins and Smith Ely Jelliffe (New York: Journal of Nervous and Mental Disease Publishing, 1914); 2nd edn., trs. Gregory C. Richter and E. James Lieberman (Baltimore: Johns Hopkins University Press, 2004).

Joseph Campbell, *The Hero with a Thousand Faces*, 1st edn. (New York: Pantheon Books, 1949).

Lord Raglan, *The Hero* (London: Methuen, 1936). Citations are from the reprint of Part 2, which is on myth, in Otto Rank et al., *In Quest of the Hero* (Princeton, NJ: Princeton University Press, 1990), pp. 89–175.

Chapter 6: Myth and psychology

Sigmund Freud, *The Interpretation of Dreams*, vols IV–V, *Standard Edition of the Complete Psychological Works of Sigmund Freud*, eds. and trs. James Strachey et al. (London: Hogarth Press and Institute of Psycho-Analysis, 1953 [1913]).

Karl Abraham, *Dreams and Myths*, tr. William A. White (New York: Journal of Nervous and Mental Disease Publishing, 1913).

Rank, *The Myth of the Birth of the Hero*, 1st edn. Citations are from the reprint in Rank et al., *In Quest of the Hero*, pp. 3–86. See also Rank's even more Oedipal *The Incest Theme in Literature and Language*, 1st edn., tr. Gregory Richter (Baltimore: Johns Hopkins University Press, 1992). See also Rank and Hanns Sachs, *The Significance of Psychoanalysis for the Mental Sciences*, tr. Charles R. Payne (New York: Nervous and Mental Disease Publishing, 1913).

On male creation myths, see Alan Dundes, 'Earth-Driver: Creation of the Mythopoeic Male', *American Anthropologist*, 64 (1962): 1032–51.

Jacob A. Arlow, 'Ego Psychology and the Study of Mythology', *Journal of the American Psychoanalytic Association*, 9 (1961): 371–93.

Bruno Bettelheim, *The Uses of Enchantment* (New York: Vintage Books, 1977 [1976]).

Géza Róheim, 'Psycho-Analysis and the Folk-Tale', *International Journal of Psycho-Analysis*, 3 (1922): 180–6; 'Myth and Folk-Tale', *American Imago*, 2 (1941): 266–79; *The Riddle of the Sphinx*, tr. R. Money-Kyrle (New York: Harper Torchbooks, 1974 [1934]); *Fire in the Dragon and Other Psychoanalytic Essays on Folklore*, ed. Alan Dundes (Princeton, NJ: Princeton University Press, 1992).

Alan Dundes, *Analytic Essays in Folklore* (The Hague: Mouton, 1975); *Interpreting Folklore* (Bloomington: Indiana University Press, 1980); *Parsing through Customs* (Madison: University of Wisconsin Press, 1987); *Folklore Matters* (Knoxville: University of Tennessee Press, 1989); *The Meaning of Folklore*, ed. Simon J. Bronner (Logan: Utah State University Press, 2007).

On creation myths, see Erich Neumann, *The Origins and History of Consciousness*, tr. R. F. C. Hull (Princeton, NJ: Princeton University Press, 1970 [1954]); Marie-Louise von Franz, *Creation Myths*, rev. edn. (Boston: Shambhala, 1995 [1st edn. (entitled *Patterns of Creativity Mirrored in Creation Myths*) 1972]).

Campbell, *The Hero with a Thousand Faces*. Citations are from the second edition (Princeton, NJ: Princeton University Press, 1968).

On Adonis, see especially C. G. Jung, *Symbols of Transformation*, *Collected Works of C. G. Jung*, eds. Sir Herbert Read et al., trs. R. F. C. Hull et al., V, 2nd edn. (Princeton, NJ: Princeton University Press, 1967 [1956]), pp. 219, 223 n. 32, 258–9, 343 n. 79.

On the archetype of the *puer aeternus*, see especially Jung, *Symbols of Transformation*, pp. 257–9, 340; 'Psychological Aspects of the Mother Archetype', in *The Archetypes and the Collective Unconscious*, *Collected Works*, IX, Part 1, 2nd edn. (Princeton, NJ: Princeton University Press, 1968 [1959]), p. 106; Marie-Louise von Franz, *Puer aeternus*, 2nd edn. (Santa Monica, CA: Sigo, 1981 [1st edn. 1970]).

On the archetype of the Great Mother, see especially Jung, 'Psychological Aspects of the Mother Archetype', pp. 75–110; *Symbols of Transformation*, pp. 207–444.

Myth

Chapter 7: Myth and structure

Claude Lévi-Strauss, 'The Structural Study of Myth', *Journal of American Folklore*, 68 (1955): 428–44, reprinted in *Myth: A Symposium*, ed. Thomas A. Sebeok (Bloomington: Indiana University Press, 1958), paperback (1965); also reprinted, slightly revised, in Lévi-Strauss, *Structural Anthropology*, trs. Claire Jacobson and Brooke Grundfest Schoepf (New York: Basic Books, 1963), chapter 11. Citations are from the Sebeok paperback. *Introduction to a Science of Mythology*, trs. John and Doreen Weightman, 4 vols (New York: Harper & Row, 1969–81), paperback (New York: Harper Torchbooks, 1970–82). Citations are from the paperback. The volumes are individually named: *The Raw and the Cooked*, *From Honey to Ashes*, *The Origin of Table Manners*, and *The Naked Man*. 'The Study of Asdiwal', tr. Nicholas Mann, in *The Structural Study of Myth and Totemism*, ed. Edmund Leach (London: Tavistock, 1967), pp. 1–47. André Akoun et al., 'A Conversation with Claude Lévi-Strauss'.

On Lévi-Strauss' myth-ritualism, see 'The Structural Study of Myth'; 'Structure and Dialectics', in his *Structural Anthropology*, chapter 12; 'Comparative Religions of Nonliterate Peoples', in his *Structural Anthropology*, II, tr. Monique Layton (New York: Basic Books, 1976), chapter 5.

Vladimir Propp, *Morphology of the Folktale*; Georges Dumézil, *Archaic Roman Religion*, tr. Philip Krapp, 2 vols (Chicago: University of Chicago Press, 1970).

Jean-Pierre Vernant, *Myth and Thought among the Greeks*, tr. not given (London and Boston: Routledge & Kegan Paul, 1983); Vernant and Pierre Vidal-Naquet, *Myth and Tragedy in Ancient Greece*, tr. Janet Lloyd (Brighton: Harvester Press, 1981); Nicole Loraux, *The Invention of Athens*, tr. Alan Sheridan (Cambridge, MA: Harvard University Press, 1987).

Marcel Detienne, *The Gardens of Adonis*, tr. Janet Lloyd (Hassock: Harvester Press; Atlantic Highlands, NJ: Humanities Press, 1977).

Chapter 8: Myth and politics

For the extreme view that all myths are political, see Robert Ellwood, *The Politics of Myth* (Albany: State University of New York Press, 1999); Bruce Lincoln, *Theorizing Myth* (Chicago: University of Chicago Press, 2000).

Malinowski, 'Myth in Primitive Psychology'.

Georges A. Sorel, *Reflections on Violence*, trs. T. E. Hulme and J. Roth (New York: Collier Books; London: Collier-Macmillan, 1961 [1950]).

Stefan Arvidsson, *Aryan Idols*, tr. Sonia Wichmann (Chicago: University of Chicago Press, 2006 [2000]).

On national myths, see Henry Nash Smith, *Virgin Land* (Cambridge, MA: Harvard University Press, 1950); Richard T. Hughes, *Myths America Lives By* (Urbana: University of Illinois Press, 2004); George S. Williamson, *The Longing for Myth in Germany* (Chicago: University of Chicago Press, 2004); Geoffrey Hosking and George Schöpflin, eds., *Myths and Nationhood* (London: Hurst, 1997).

On myth and ideology, see Ben Halpern, ' "Myth" and "Ideology" in Modern Usage', *History and Theory*, 1 (1961): 129–49; Christopher G. Flood, *Political Myth* (New York: Routledge, 2001 [1996]).

Ernst Cassirer, *The Myth of the State* (New Haven, CT: Yale University Press, 1946); *Symbol, Myth, and Culture*, ed. Donald Phillip Verene (New Haven, CT: Yale University Press, 1979), pp. 219–67.

Dumézil, *Archaic Roman Religion*; *Mitra-Varuna*, tr. Derek Cottman (New York: Zone Books, 1988 [1948]); *Gods of the Ancient Northmen*, ed. Einar Haigen (Berkeley: University of California, 1973 [1959]).

Girard, *Violence and the Sacred*.

On matriarchy in Greece and elsewhere, see, classically, J. J. Bachofen, *Myth, Religion, and Mother Right*, tr. Ralph Manheim (Princeton, NJ: Princeton University Press, 1967).

Herodotus, *The Histories*, tr. Aubrey de Sélincourt, rev. and ed. A. R. Burn (Harmondsworth: Penguin, 1972 [1954]).

Aristotle, *Constitution of Athens and Related Texts*, trs. Kurt von Fritz and Ernst Kapp (New York: Hafner Press, 1974 [1950]).

Pierre Vidal-Naquet, 'The Black Hunter and the Origin of the Athenian Ephebeia', in *Myth, Religion and Society*, ed. R. L. Gordon (Cambridge: Cambridge University Press, 1981), pp. 147–62.

Conclusion: bringing myth back to the world

James Lovelock, *Gaia: A New Look at Life on Earth* (Oxford and New York: Oxford University Press, 1979); reprinted with new preface (2000); *The Ages of Gaia* (1988 [2nd edn. 1995]); *Gaia: Medicine for an Ailing Planet*, rev. edn. (London: Gaia Books, 2005) [1st edn. 1991]); *The Revenge of Gaia* (London: Penguin Books, 2007 [2006]).

Index

Myth

Myth

ONLINE CATALOGUE
A Very Short Introduction

Our online catalogue is designed to make it easy to find your ideal Very Short Introduction. View the entire collection by subject area, watch author videos, read sample chapters, and download reading guides.

http://fds.oup.com/www.oup.co.uk/general/vsi/index.html

SOCIAL MEDIA
Very Short Introduction

Join our community
www.oup.com/vsi

- Join us online at the official Very Short Introductions **Facebook** page.
- Access the thoughts and musings of our authors with our online **blog**.
- Sign up for our monthly **e-newsletter** to receive information on all new titles publishing that month.
- Browse the full range of Very Short Introductions online.
- Read **extracts** from the Introductions for free.
- Visit our library of **Reading Guides**. These guides, written by our expert authors will help you to question again, why you think what you think.
- If you are a teacher or lecturer you can order inspection copies quickly and simply via our website.